THE BOOK OF
Hot & Spicy
FOODS

THE BOOK OF

Hot & Spicy
FOODS

LOUISE STEELE

Photography by
PAUL GRATER

HPBooks

ANOTHER BEST SELLING VOLUME FROM HPBooks

Published by HPBooks, a division of Price Stern Sloan, Inc.
360 N. La Cienega Blvd., Los Angeles, CA 90048
9 8 7 6 5 4 3 2

By arrangement with Salamander Books Ltd. and Merehurst Press, London.

Photography: Paul Grater
Home Economist: Anne Hildyard
Color separation by J. Film Process Ltd., Bangkok, Thailand
Printed in Belgium by Proost International Book Production
Typeset by Angel Graphics

Library of Congress Cataloging-in-Publication Data

Steele, Louise, 1945—
    The book of hot & spicy foods.

    Includes index.
    1. Cookery, International.   2. Spices.   I. Title.
II. Title: Book of hot and spicy foods.
TX725.A1S655   1987   641.6'384   87-11917
ISBN 0-89586-642-0

CONTENTS

LOUISE STEELE

Louise Steele has a wide range of experience in writing magazine articles and books throughout the world. She is a cookery writer and editor for several publications. A trained home economist, she has authored several cookbooks.

INTRODUCTION

Variety is said to be the spice of life and, whereas for many millions of people throughout the world, life has been a variety of spices for centuries, it's only thanks to early explorers, who returned home with shiploads of exotic spices, that Western culinary art was transformed.

The Book of Hot & Spicy Foods has a collection of over 100 beautifully illustrated step-by-step recipes which include traditional favorites like Steak au Poivre, Mexican Chili con Carne, Indonesian Gado Gado and Creole Jambalaya, plus many Indian and Oriental dishes and lots of sizzling new surprises and variations on a theme. Whether it's a simple snack, a teatime treat or an elegant dinner party dish you're after, this book has a recipe for all occasions.

Spices are invaluable for adding that special blend of heat or fragrance and pungency to all manner of savory and sweet dishes. Don't be daunted by those unfamiliar to you—try them, or you'll never know what you've been missing, but bear in mind that some are stronger and fierier than others. If experimenting, it is wise to start with small amounts—you can always add more to taste at a later stage. And remember—the amount of spices in many of the following recipes are suggested as a guide, so feel free to increase or decrease the amounts according to personal preference.

It is the chili (in its various forms) that adds heat to a dish. You will find instructions on how to prepare this fiery spice (without getting burnt!), plus many recipes using it. There is also plenty of information on all the other hot spices—mustard, pepper, cloves and ginger—plus, of course, the more fragrant, aromatic ones like cardamom, cumin, nutmeg, etc. And no spice book would be complete without recipes for making Curry Powder, Garam Masala, Five Spice Powder, Mixed Spice, Pickling Spice and Harissa (a Middle Eastern favorite).

The following recipes range from mild to hot or just wonderfully spicy. It is surely a collection to please not only hot and spicy food-lovers everywhere, but also tempting enough to persuade the "uninitiated" to sample the delights of spicy foods!

CHILIES

Chilies belong to the capsicum family, as do sweet peppers, but there the relationship ends, for the fiery heat of the chili is in no way similar to its mild-flavored relation. Fresh chilies are now widely available and vary considerably in size, shape and heat factor. In principle, the fatter chilies tend to be more mild than the long, thin varieties, and the smaller the chili, the hotter its taste. Generally, the unripened, green chili is less fiery than when ripened and red. This is a useful guide to follow, but there are exceptions according to the variety, so it is wise to remember that all chilies, irrespective of color, shape and size, are hot, so use caution before adding them to a dish. Bear in mind that a little chili goes a long way, so add a small amount to begin with and gradually increase the quantity to your liking during cooking.

Take care when preparing chilies—the tiny, cream-colored seeds inside are the hottest part and, in general, are removed before using. Chilies contain a pungent oil which can cause an unpleasant burning sensation to eyes and skin, so it's a wise precaution to wear rubber gloves when handling chilies and to be sure not to touch your face or eyes during preparation. Cut off the stalk end, then split open the pod and scrape out seeds, using a pointed knife, and discard. Rinse pod thoroughly with cold running water and pat chili dry before chopping or slicing as required. Once this task is completed, always wash your hands, utensils and surfaces thoroughly with soapy water.

Dried red chilies are sold whole and can vary in size from 1/2-3/4 to 1-1/2-2 inches in length, so take this into account when using. If a recipe states small dried chilies, and you only have the larger ones, adapt and lessen the quantity accordingly, or to taste. Dried chilies are usually soaked in hot water for 1 hour before draining and removing seeds (as described above), unless a recipe states otherwise.

Dried red chilies, when ground, are used to make cayenne pepper and, combined with other spices and seasonings, also make chili and curry powder, and chili seasoning. They are also used in the making of hot-pepper sauce and chili sauces.

The Harissa spice mix, page 13, uses a large quantity of dried chilies and is very hot, so be forewarned! This is a favorite spice mix for many Middle Eastern dishes. Don't be tempted to add more Harissa than recipe states, unless you are prepared for an extremely hot dish. A less fiery Harissa can be made simply by removing the seeds from soaked chilies before crushing chilies with other ingredients.

Green chilies are available canned. These are often seeded and peeled and taste pleasantly hot and spicy—ideal for adding to pizza toppings, sauces and taco fillings. Both red and green chilies also come pickled in jars (hot or mild/sweet) and can be found in delicatessens and ethnic food shops. Canned and pickled varieties should be drained and patted dry before using. Whether you seed the pickled type is up to you, just remember the seeds are the hottest part!

MUSTARD

White or yellow, brown and black seeds come from the mustard plant, according to the species. Most commonly found is the creamy yellow type which is the least pungent. The brown type (or Indian mustard) is stronger in flavor, while the black mustard seed is the most powerful of all. The creamy yellow seeds are more widely available, but look for the black and brown types in Asian and Oriental food shops and delicatessens.

Whole mustard seeds have a pleasant nutty bite to them and can be used to add piquancy to salad dressing and hot sauces. They are especially good when served with fish, chicken and pork and are also delicious added to cole slaw, creamy potato salads, pickles and chutneys. Use mustard seeds (especially the two hotter varieties) with discretion to begin with, increasing the amount as you become more familiar with the flavors.

It is the yellow seed which, when processed with black seeds, wheat flour and turmeric, forms the basis of English mustard. Dry mustard can be used as it is in cooking, or it may be mixed to a paste with a little cold or warm water. (For a nice rich mixture, why not try mixing it with a little cream or milk?) Once mixed it should be left at least 10 minutes to allow time for the flavors to develop. It is only when the powder is mixed with a liquid that the essential oils are released, giving mustard its pungency and sensation of heat. Remember that made mustard loses its pungency after a few hours. Jars of prepared mustards, once opened, need using within a few weeks as the flavor and color will deteriorate.

The variety of ready-prepared mustards come in a bewildering number of mouthwatering flavors, according to the manufacturer. These can be made from milled mustard flour, or from coarsely crushed seed (the proportions of which vary tremendously, depending on the type). Some are mixed with vinegar, others with grape juice or wine (and sometimes beer), and often contain various spices, herbs and seasonings, such as honey and horseradish. German mustard, which is mild and sweet-flavored, is a mixture of brown and white mustard flour moistened with vinegar and flavored with various spices. The mild-flavored American mustard (popular with children) generally uses only yellow mustard seeds with the addition of sugar, vinegar and salt. Dijon-style mustard, made from milled, husked black seeds, is flavored with wine and spices. The pungent and spicy grainy types of mustard are a mixture of whole, crushed black and yellow seeds with additional flavorings added for individuality.

Mustards of all types can be used to great effect, not only as a condiment, but also as a culinary ingredient. They add bite and piquancy to all types of savory dishes from scrambled eggs, sauces and dressings to deviled mixtures, barbecued food, soups, casseroles, pastry, scones and cheesy biscuits.

A to Z OF SPICES

ALLSPICE (1): These small dark, reddish-brown berries are so called because their aroma and flavor resemble a combination of cinnamon, cloves and nutmeg. Use berries whole in marinades; for boiling and pot roasting meats and poultry; in fish dishes, pickles and chutneys. Also available ground and excellent for flavoring soups, sauces and desserts.

ANISE (2): Commonly called aniseed, these small, brown oval seeds have the sweet, pungent flavor of licorice. Also available ground. Use seeds in stews and vegetable dishes, or sprinkle over loaves and rolls before baking. Try ground anise for flavoring fish dishes and pastries for fruit pies.

CARAWAY (3): Small brown, crescent-shaped seeds with a strong liquorice flavor and especially delicious as a flavoring in braised cabbage and sauerkraut recipes, breads (particularly rye), cakes and cheeses.

CARDAMOM (4): Small, triangular-shaped pods containing numerous small black seeds which have a warm, highly aromatic flavor. You can buy green or black cardamoms although the smaller green type is more widely available.

CAYENNE (5): Orangey-red in color, this ground pepper is extremely hot and pungent. Not to be confused with paprika which, although related, is mild-flavored.

CHILI POWDER (6): Made from dried red chilies. This red powder varies in flavor and hotness, from mild to hot. A less fiery type is found in chili seasoning.

CINNAMON (7) & CASSIA (8): Shavings of bark from the cinnamon tree are processed and curled to form cinnamon sticks. Also available in ground form. Spicy, fragrant and sweet, it is used widely in savory and sweet dishes. Cassia (from the dried bark of the cassia tree) is similar to cinnamon, but less delicate in flavor with a slight pungent 'bite'.

CLOVES (9): These dried, unopened flower buds give a warm aroma and pungency to foods, but should be used with care as the flavor can become overpowering. Available in ground form. Cloves are added to soups, sauces, mulled drinks, stewed fruits and apple pies.

CORIANDER (10): Available in seed and ground form. These tiny, pale brown seeds have a mild, spicy flavor with a slight orange peel fragrance. An essential spice in curry dishes, but also extremely good in many cake and cookie recipes.

CUMIN (11): Sold in seed or ground. Cumin has a warm, pungent aromatic flavor and is used extensively to flavor curries and many Middle Eastern and Mexican dishes. Popular in Germany for flavoring sauerkraut and pork dishes. Use ground or whole in meat dishes and stuffed vegetables.

FENUGREEK (12): These small, yellow-brown seeds have a slight bitter flavor which, when added in small quantities, is very good in curries, chutneys and pickles, soups, fish and shellfish dishes.

GINGER (13): Available in many forms. Invaluable for adding to many savory and sweet dishes and for baking gingerbread and brandy snaps. Fresh ginger root looks like a knobby stem. It should be peeled and finely chopped or sliced before use. Dried ginger root is very hard and light beige in color. To release flavor, "bruise" with a spoon or soak in hot water before using. This dried type is more often used in pickling, jam making and preserving. Also available in ground form, preserved stem ginger and crystallized ginger.

MACE (14) & NUTMEG (15): Both are found on the same plant. The nutmeg is the inner kernel of the fruit. When ripe, the fruit splits open to reveal bright red arils which lie around the shell of the nutmeg—and once dried are known as mace blades. The flavor of both spices is very similar—warm, sweet and aromatic, although nutmeg is more delicate than mace. Both spices are also sold ground. Use with vegetables; sprinkled over egg dishes, milk puddings and custards; eggnogs and mulled drinks; or use as a flavoring in desserts.

PAPRIKA (16): Comes from a variety of pepper (capsicum) and although similar in color to cayenne, this bright red powder has a mild flavor.

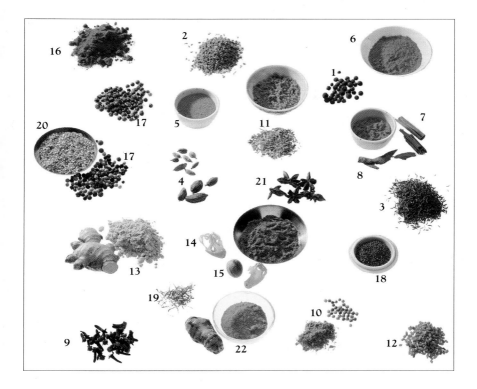

PEPPER (17): White pepper comes from ripened berries with the outer husks removed. Black pepper comes from unripened berries dried until dark greenish-black in color. Black pepper is more subtle than white. Use white or black peppercorns in marinades and pickling, or freshly ground as a seasoning. Both are available ground. Green peppercorns are also unripe berries with a mild, light flavor. They are canned in brine or pickled, or freeze-dried in jars. They add a pleasant, light peppery flavor to sauces, pâtés and salad dressings. Drain those packed in liquid and use either whole or mash them lightly before using. Dry green peppercorns should be lightly crushed before using to help release flavor, unless otherwise stated in a recipe.

POPPY SEEDS (18): These tiny, slate-blue seeds add a nutty flavor to both sweet and savory dishes. Sprinkle over desserts and breads.

SAFFRON (19): This spice comes from the stigmas of a species of crocus. It has a distinctive flavor and gives a rich yellow coloring to dishes, however, it is also the most expensive spice to buy. Available in small packets or jars (either powdered or in strands—the strands being far superior in flavor). This spice is a must for an authentic paella or Cornish Saffron Cake. Also an extremely good flavoring for soups, fish and chicken dishes.

SESAME SEEDS (20): High in protein and mineral oil content, sesame seeds have a crisp texture and sweet, nutty flavor which combines well in curries and with chicken, pork and fish dishes. Use also to sprinkle over breads, cookies and pastries before baking.

STAR ANISE (21): This dried, star-shaped seed head has a pungent, aromatic smell, rather similar to fennel. Use very sparingly in stir-fry dishes. Also good with fish and poultry.

TURMERIC (22): Closely related to ginger, it is an aromatic root which is dried and ground to produce a bright, orange-yellow powder. It has a rich, warm, distinctive smell, a delicate, aromatic flavor and helps give dishes an attractive yellow coloring. Use in curries, fish and shellfish dishes, rice pilafs and lentil mixtures. It is also a necessary ingredient in mustard pickles and piccalilli.

All spices should be stored in small airtight jars in a cool, dark place, as heat, moisture and sunlight reduce their flavor.

GARAM MASALA

10 green or 6 black cardamoms, pods
  cracked, seeded
1 tablespoon black peppercorns
2 teaspoons cumin seeds
1/2 teaspoon coriander seeds
2 small dried red chilies, seeded

Using a blender, process all ingredients
until finely ground. Store in an airtight jar
up to 3 months.

CURRY POWDER

2 tablespoons cumin seeds
2 tablespoons fenugreek
1-1/2 teaspoons mustard seeds
1 tablespoon black peppercorns
1/2 cup coriander seeds
1 tablespoon poppy seeds
1 tablespoon ground ginger
1-1/2 teaspoons hot chili powder
1/4 cup ground turmeric

Using a blender, process cumin, fenugreek, mustard, peppercorns, coriander
and poppy seeds. Add remaining spices;
process. Store up to 3 months.

FIVE SPICE POWDER

5 teaspoons ground anise (aniseed)
5 teaspoons star anise
1 (5-inch) cinnamon stick or equivalent
  in cassia bark
2 tablespoons whole cloves
7 teaspoons fennel seeds

Using a blender, process all ingredients
until finely ground. Store in an airtight jar
up to 3 months.

MIXED SPICE

1 (3-inch) cinnamon stick, broken in
  small pieces
2-1/2 teaspoons allspice berries
1 tablespoon whole cloves
2 teaspoons freshly grated nutmeg
1 tablespoon ground ginger

Using a coffee grinder or blender, process
cinnamon, allspice berries and cloves until
very finely ground. Add to freshly grated
nutmeg and ginger and mix well. Store in a
small, airtight jar up to 1 month.

PICKLING SPICE

2 tablespoons mace blades
1 tablespoon allspice berries
1 tablespoon whole cloves
2 (3-inch) cinnamon sticks, broken into
  small pieces
12 black peppercorns
1 dried bay leaf, crumbled

In a small bowl, mix all ingredients. Store
in a small, airtight jar up to 2 months.

HARISSA

1 ounce dried red chilies
1 clove garlic, chopped
1 teaspoon caraway seeds
1 teaspoon cumin seeds
1 teaspoon coriander seeds
Several pinches salt
Olive oil

Soak chilies in hot water 1 hour. Drain
well; pat dry. Grind to a smooth paste with
garlic, spices and salt. Add enough olive
oil to cover surface. Cover and store in a
cool place up to 2 months.

— MARINATED SPICED OLIVES —

3/4 cup pitted ripe olives
3/4 cup pimento-stuffed green olives
3 lemon slices
3 dried red chilies
2 garlic cloves, crushed
1 teaspoon mustard seeds
1 teaspoon black peppercorns
3 allspice berries
About 1-3/4 cups olive oil

Drain any brine from olives. Put olives into a bowl.

Add lemon slices, chilies, garlic, mustard seeds, peppercorns and allspice berries. Stir in olive oil and mix well. Spoon mixture into a large jar with a tight-fitting lid. Screw on lid tightly and turn jar over several times to ensure ingredients are well mixed.

Let olives marinate at least 1 week before serving, turning jar several times a day. Store up to 6 months in a cool place. Makes 4 to 6 servings.

NOTE: Use a mixture of corn oil and olive oil for a more economical marinade. Add sprigs of dried herbs to marinade, if desired. To serve, garnish with lemon twists and a fresh parsley sprig, if desired.

– CHEESY MUSHROOM CANAPÉS –

2 tablespoons butter
4 ounces mushrooms, coarsely
  chopped
4 teaspoons all-purpose flour
2 cups (8 ounces) shredded Cheddar
  cheese
1 teaspoon mustard powder
1 teaspoon Worcestershire sauce
Freshly ground pepper to taste
8 (about 3/4-inch-thick) slices French
  bread
1 to 2 tablespoons chopped fresh
  parsley
Paprika
Fresh parsley sprigs, if desired

In a saucepan, melt butter. Add mushrooms and cook gently 2 minutes. Add flour and stir into mushroom mixture.

Add cheese, mustard and Worcestershire sauce. Stir well and heat through gently 2 minutes or until mixture begins to melt. Remove from heat and season to taste with pepper.

Preheat broiler. Toast bread on one side only. Spread cheese and mushroom mixture on untoasted sides. Broil in preheated broiler 3 to 4 minutes or until melted and bubbling. Cut slices in half and sprinkle liberally with parsley and paprika. Garnish with parsley sprigs, if desired, and serve hot. Makes 4 servings.

— BOMBAY NUT 'N' RAISIN MIX —

2/3 cup thin pretzel sticks
3 tablespoons butter
1 clove garlic, crushed
1/3 cup unblanched almonds
1/3 cup pine nuts
1/3 cup unsalted cashews
1 teaspoon Worcestershire sauce
1 teaspoon Curry Powder, page 12
1/2 teaspoon hot chili powder
1/3 cup seedless raisins
1/4 teaspoon salt

Break pretzels into 1-inch sticks. Melt butter in a skillet.

Add garlic to butter, then stir in almonds, pine nuts and cashews. Add Worcestershire sauce, curry powder and chili powder and mix well. Stir in pretzels and cook gently over medium heat 3 to 4 minutes, stirring frequently.

Remove from heat. Add raisins and salt; mix well. Turn mixture into a serving dish and cool. Makes about 2 cups.

COCKTAIL KEBABS

8 cooked large shrimp
2 green onions, trimmed
1/2 red bell pepper, seeded, cut in thin
  strips and decorative shapes
8 small ripe or green olives
1 clove garlic, crushed
2 tablespoons lemon juice
2 tablespoons olive oil
1 teaspoon sugar
1 teaspoon coarsely ground mustard
1/4 teaspoon creamed horseradish

Remove heads and body shells from shrimp but leave on tail shells.

Devein shrimp by removing black spinal cord. Cut each green onion in 4 daisies. Put shrimp, green onions, bell pepper and olives into a bowl. Mix garlic, lemon juice, olive oil, sugar, mustard and horseradish.

Pour over shrimp mixture, cover and marinate at least 2 hours, stirring occasionally. Remove ingredients from marinade and thread equally on 8 wooden picks. Drain on paper towels. Makes 8 kebabs.

Variation: Add small slices avocado to shrimp mixture.

FILO SHRIMP PUFFS

1 tablespoon sesame oil
2 tablespoons corn oil
1 clove garlic, crushed
1 onion, finely chopped
1 (1-inch) piece ginger root, peeled,
   grated
1/2 teaspoon turmeric
1/2 teaspoon chili powder
1/4 teaspoon ground cumin
6 ounces medium-size peeled raw
   shrimp, thawed if frozen
2 tablespoons creamed coconut, diced
5 sheets filo pastry
1/4 cup butter or ghee, melted
Fresh Italian parsley sprigs, if desired

Preheat oven to 350F (175C). Lightly grease
a baking sheet. Heat sesame and corn oil in
a saucepan. Add garlic, onion and ginger.
Fry gently 5 minutes, stirring occasionally.

Add turmeric, chili powder and cumin. Fry
gently 2 minutes. Add shrimp, cover and
cook gently 5 minutes, stirring frequently.
Remove from heat, stir in creamed coconut
and cool.

Work with 1 to 2 sheets of filo pastry at a time; cover remainder with a damp cloth. Cut sheet of pastry in half lengthwise and then fold each piece in half lengthwise to make 2 long narrow strips. Spoon a portion of shrimp mixture in 1 corner of each strip of pastry. Brush pastry all over with a small amount of melted butter or ghee.

Fold pastry and filling over at right angles to make a triangle. Continue folding in this way along pastry strip to form a triangular parcel. Brush with melted butter or ghee and place on greased baking sheet. Repeat with remaining pastry and shrimp mixture.

Bake in preheated oven 20 minutes. Brush with remaining melted butter or ghee and return to oven 5 to 10 minutes or until puffs are golden brown. Garnish with parsley sprigs, if desired, and serve warm. Makes 10 puffs.

TANGY POTTED CHEESE

4 ounces Cheddar cheese
1/4 cup butter, softened
1 tablespoon port or sherry
4 green onions, finely chopped
1/2 teaspoon caraway seeds
1/2 to 1 teaspoon coarsely ground
mustard
1/4 teaspoon Worcestershire sauce
1/4 cup walnuts, coarsely chopped
Crackers or melba toast
Fresh parsley sprigs, if desired

Finely grate cheese into a bowl. Add butter and mix well.

Stir in port, green onions, caraway seeds, mustard and Worcestershire sauce. Mix thoroughly until well combined.

Spoon mixture into a serving dish. Cover with walnuts and press walnuts down lightly into mixture. Chill at least 2 hours. Serve with crisp crackers or Melba toast and garnish with parsley sprigs, if desired. Makes 4 to 6 servings.

Variation: Add 1 teaspoon chopped fresh herbs and a few pinches cayenne pepper to taste.

NOTE: This spread will keep in refrigerator up to 5 days.

PIQUANT POPCORN

2 tablespoons corn oil
2 cloves garlic, crushed
1 (1/2-inch) piece ginger root, peeled, chopped
1 cup popping corn
1/4 cup butter
2 teaspoons hot chili sauce
2 tablespoons chopped fresh parsley
Salt to taste

Heat oil in a saucepan. Add 1 clove of crushed garlic, ginger and popping corn. Stir well.

Cover and cook over medium-high heat 3 to 5 minutes, holding lid firmly and shaking pan frequently until popping stops. Turn popped corn into a dish, discarding any unpopped corn kernels. Melt butter in pan. Stir in remaining clove of crushed garlic and chili sauce.

Return corn to pan and toss well until evenly coated with mixture. Add parsley and salt and stir well. Turn into a serving dish. Serve warm or cold. Makes 6 to 8 servings.

Variation: Omit chili sauce and add 1 teaspoon dry mustard, 1 teaspoon paprika, 1/2 teaspoon ground coriander and 2 tablespoons chopped fresh chives to melted butter.

CHEESE CHILI BITES

1 cup all-purpose flour
1/4 teaspoon salt
1/2 teaspoon dry mustard
1/4 to 1/2 teaspoon hot chili powder
Large pinch cayenne pepper
1/4 cup butter or margarine
1/2 cup (2 oz.) finely grated Cheddar
  cheese
1 egg, beaten
1 tablespoon cold water
1 tablespoon sesame seeds
1 tablespoon poppy seeds

Preheat oven to 400F (205C). Sift flour, salt and spices into a bowl.

Cut in butter finely until mixture resembles breadcrumbs. Add grated cheese and mix well. Mix egg with cold water. Add 2 tablespoons of egg mixture to cheese mixture and mix to form a fairly stiff dough. Knead gently on a lightly floured surface. Roll out dough to a 12" x 6" rectangle. Trim edges. Cut in half lengthwise and transfer to a baking sheet.

Brush each half with remaining egg mixture. Sprinkle 1 half with sesame seeds and the other half with poppy seeds. Cut each half in 10 triangles and separate slightly to prevent sticking. Bake in preheated oven 10 to 12 minutes or until light golden and cooked through. Cool on a wire rack. Store in an airtight container up to 2 weeks. Makes 20 appetizers.

— PEPPERY MOZZARELLA SALAD —

6 ounces Mozzarella cheese
2 large beefsteak tomatoes, cut in half
1 ripe avocado
2 shallots, peeled, thinly sliced
1/3 cup olive oil
2 tablespoons lemon juice
1/2 teaspoon sugar
Salt to taste
1/4 to 1/2 teaspoon dry mustard
1 to 2 teaspoons green peppercorns,
   crushed
1/2 teaspoon dried oregano
Crusty bread or bread sticks

Thinly slice cheese and tomato and arrange on 4 small plates.

Cut avocado in thin slices and arrange with cheese and tomato. Separate shallots in rings and scatter over salad.

In a screw-topped jar, combine olive oil, lemon juice, sugar, salt, peppercorns and oregano. Shake vigorously until well blended. Spoon over salad and let marinate 1 hour. Garnish with basil, if desired, and serve with warm crusty bread or bread sticks. Makes 4 servings.

– CURRIED CHICKEN LIVER PÂTÉ –

3/4 cup butter
1 onion, finely chopped
1 garlic clove, chopped
8 ounces chicken livers
1 to 2 teaspoons Curry Powder,
    page 12
1/2 cup chicken stock
2 hard-boiled eggs, shelled
Salt and freshly ground pepper to taste
2 pinches cayenne pepper
Fresh bay leaves, if desired
Lemon pieces, if desired
Crusty bread

Melt 1/2 of butter in a skillet. Add onion, garlic and chicken livers and cook gently 5 minutes, stirring constantly.

Stir in curry powder and cook 1 minute. Add chicken stock and cook gently 5 minutes, stirring and turning livers frequently. In a blender or food processor, process chicken liver mixture and hard-boiled eggs to a smooth purée.

Add salt, pepper and cayenne pepper. Turn mixture into a serving dish or terrine. Smooth surface. Melt remaining butter in a saucepan and pour over surface of pâté. Let set slightly, then garnish with bay leaves and lemon pieces, if desired. Chill several hours or overnight before serving with bread. Makes 6 servings.

Variation: Add curry powder to taste to melted butter topping.

—— MUSSEL & SAFFRON SOUP ——

2 pounds mussels
1-1/4 cups dry white wine
1-1/2 cups water
3 tablespoons butter
1 tablespoon olive oil
1 onion, finely chopped
1 garlic clove, crushed
1 leek, trimmed, finely shredded
1/2 teaspoon fenugreek, finely crushed
1-1/2 tablespoons all-purpose flour
2 (0.05 gram) packets saffron strands,
   soaked in 1 tablespoon
   boiling water
1-1/4 cups chicken stock
1 tablespoon chopped fresh parsley
Salt and freshly ground pepper to taste
2 tablespoons whipping cream
Fresh parsley sprigs, if desired

Scrub mussels clean in several changes of fresh water and pull off beards. Discard any mussels that are cracked or do not close tightly when tapped. Put mussels into a saucepan with wine and water. Cover and cook over high heat, shaking pan frequently, 6 to 7 minutes or until shells open. Remove mussels, discarding any which remain closed. Strain liquid through a fine sieve and reserve.

Heat butter and oil in a saucepan. Add onion, garlic, leek and fenugreek and cook gently 5 minutes. Stir in flour and cook 1 minute. Add saffron mixture, 2-1/2 cups of reserved cooking liquid and chicken stock. Bring to a boil, cover and simmer gently 15 minutes. Meanwhile, keep 8 mussels in shells and remove remaining mussels from shells. Add all mussels to soup and stir in chopped parsley, salt, pepper and cream. Heat through 2 to 3 minutes. Garnish with parsley sprigs, if desired, and serve hot. Makes 4 servings.

—— CHILIED RED BEAN DIP ——

2 tablespoons corn oil
1 clove garlic, crushed
1 onion, finely chopped
1 fresh green chili, seeded, finely
 chopped
1 teaspoon hot chili powder
1 (15-oz.) can red kidney beans
1/2 cup (2 oz.) shredded Cheddar
 cheese
Salt to taste
Thin slivers fresh red and green chilies
Fresh parsley sprig, if desired
Tortilla chips

Heat oil in a skillet. Add garlic, onion, green chili and chili powder and cook gently 4 minutes.

Drain kidney beans, reserving juice. Reserve 3 tablespoons beans; process remainder in a blender or food processor to a purée. Add to onion mixture and stir in 2 tablespoons of reserved bean liquid; mix well.

Stir in reserved beans and cheese. Cook gently about 2 minutes, stirring until cheese melts. Add salt and mix well. If mixture becomes too thick, add a little more reserved bean liquid. Spoon into a serving dish and garnish with chilies and parsley sprig, if desired. Serve warm with tortilla chips. Makes 4 to 6 servings.

—— SPICED MELON COCKTAIL ——

1 ripe honeydew melon, cut in half,
  seeded
1-1/2 cups whipping cream
1-1/2 cups mayonnaise
2 teaspoons lemon juice
1 teaspoon paprika
1/2 teaspoon hot-pepper sauce
1/2 teaspoon Worcestershire sauce
2 tablespoons tomato paste
8 ounces white crabmeat, flaked
8 radicchio leaves, shredded
Lemon and lime slices, if desired
Fresh mint sprigs, if desired

Scoop melon in balls.

To make dressing, whip cream until soft
peaks form. Mix in mayonnaise, lemon
juice, paprika, hot-pepper sauce, Worcestershire sauce and tomato paste.

Stir crabmeat into dressing. Lightly mix in
melon and toss ingredients gently until
coated. Arrange shredded radicchio on 4
individual serving dishes. Spoon melon
and crab mixture on radicchio. Chill lightly. To serve, garnish with citrus slices and
mint sprigs, if desired. Makes 4 servings.

─── VEGETABLE SAMOSA ───

8 ounces potatoes, cut in even-size
   pieces
3/4 cup frozen green peas
2 tablespoons corn oil
1 onion, finely chopped
1/2 teaspoon cumin seeds
1 (1/2-inch) piece ginger root, peeled,
   grated
1/2 teaspoon tumeric
1/2 teaspoon Garam Masala, page 12
1/2 teaspoon salt
2 teaspoons lemon juice
1 cup all-purpose flour
2 tablespoons butter
2 tablespoons warm milk
Vegetable oil for deep frying
Lime twists, if desired
Fresh celery leaves, if desired
Mango Chutney, page 89

In a saucepan, boil potatoes in salted water
15 to 20 minutes or until tender. Drain
well, return to saucepan and shake over
low heat a few moments or until dry. Mash
well. Cook peas in boiling salted water 4
minutes. Drain well.

Heat oil in a skillet. Add onion, cumin
seeds, ginger, turmeric, Garam Masala
and salt. Cook gently 5 minutes. Add
mashed potatoes and peas, then stir in
lemon juice. Mix well, remove from heat
and cool.

Sift flour into a bowl. Cut in butter finely until mixture resembles bread crumbs. Add milk and mix to form a stiff dough. Divide in 6 equal pieces.

Form each piece in a ball and roll each ball on a lightly floured surface to a 6-inch circle. Cut each circle in half. Divide filling equally among semicircles of pastry.

Dampen edges of pastry, then fold over and seal to form triangles which enclose filling completely. Half fill a deep-fat fryer or saucepan with oil. Heat oil to 375F (190C) or until a 1/2-inch cube of day-old bread browns in 40 seconds. Fry samosa in hot oil, a few at a time, 3 to 4 minutes or until golden brown. Drain on paper towels. Garnish with lime twists and celery leaves, if desired, and serve hot with Mango Chutney. Makes 12 samosa.

—— EGGPLANT TAHINI PÂTÉ ——

1 large eggplant
1 large clove garlic
3 shallots
1/2 to 1 teaspoon Garam Masala,
  page 12
3 tablespoons tahini (creamed sesame)
Finely grated peel 1 lemon
3 tablespoons lemon juice
Salt to taste
2 teaspoons olive oil
Cayenne pepper
Lemon slices, if desired, cut in half
Fresh parsley sprig, if desired
Pita bread, cut in strips

Preheat oven to 350F (175C). Prick egg-plant several times with a fork.

Bake eggplant in preheated oven 30 to 40 minutes or until softened and skin has turned dark brown. Cool, trim ends and peel eggplant. Process flesh in a blender or food processor with garlic, shallots, Garam Masala, tahini, lemon peel and juice until smooth and evenly combined.

Season with salt. Spoon mixture into a serving bowl, drizzle with olive oil and sprinkle with cayenne pepper. Garnish with lemon slices and parsley sprig, if de-sired, and serve with pita bread. Makes 4 to 6 servings.

— ONION & MUSHROOM BHAJIS —

1 onion
2 ounces button mushrooms
1/4 cup brown rice flour
1/4 cup all-purpose flour
1/2 teaspoon turmeric
1/2 teaspoon hot chili powder
1/4 teaspoon ground cumin
1/4 teaspoon ground coriander
1/4 teaspoon salt
2/3 cup plain yogurt
Vegetable oil for deep frying
Fresh parsley sprig, if desired

Peel, quarter and thinly slice onion.

Coarsely chop mushrooms. In a bowl, combine flours, turmeric, chili powder, cumin, coriander and salt. Stir in onion, mushrooms and yogurt; mix well.

Half fill a deep-fat fryer or saucepan with oil; heat to 375F (190C) or until a 1/2-inch cube of day-old bread browns in 40 seconds. Divide mixture in 10 equal portions. Drop spoonfuls of mixture into hot oil and fry 3 to 4 minutes or until golden brown and cooked through. Drain on paper towels. Garnish with parsley sprig, if desired, and serve warm. Makes 10 ·appetizers.

DEVILED TOMATOES

4 firm tomatoes
2 tablespoons butter
1 small clove garlic, crushed
1/2 cup fresh white bread crumbs
1 tablespoon chopped fresh parsley
1/4 teaspoon cayenne pepper
1/2 teaspoon paprika
1/4 teaspoon dry mustard
1 tablespoon grated Parmesan cheese
Salt to taste
Fresh parsley sprigs

Preheat oven to 350F (175C). Grease a 9-inch-square baking pan. Cut 1/3 slice off top of each tomato.

Reserve tops for 'lids'. Remove seeds from each tomato. Melt butter in a saucepan. Add garlic, bread crumbs and chopped parsley; mix well.

Remove from heat. Add cayenne pepper, paprika, mustard, cheese and salt; mix well. Spoon into tomatoes and form in neat mounds, pressing gently in shape with fingertips. Put reserved 'lids' on top. Arrange tomatoes, cut-sides up, in greased pan. Bake in preheated oven 15 minutes. Garnish with parley sprigs and serve hot. Makes 4 servings.

— ORIENTAL GINGERED SHRIMP —

8 unshelled raw jumbo shrimp,
   thawed if frozen
1/2 cup all-purpose flour
1/4 teaspoon salt
1 teaspoon corn oil
1/4 cup water
1 (1-inch) piece ginger root, peeled,
   grated
1 clove garlic, crushed
1 teaspoon chili sauce
1 egg white
Vegetable oil
1 green onion daisy
Red bell pepper strips

Shell shrimp, leaving tail shells on. Make a small incision along spines. Remove black spinal cord from shrimp.

In a bowl, combine flour, salt, corn oil and water. Stir in ginger, garlic and chili sauce and beat well. Stiffly whisk egg white, then gently fold into batter until evenly combined.

Half fill a deep-fat fryer or saucepan with oil; heat to 375F (190C) or until a 1/2-inch cube of day-old bread browns in 40 seconds. Hold each shrimp by its tail and dip into batter, then lower into hot oil. Fry 3 minutes or until golden. Drain on paper towels. Garnish with green onion daisy and bell pepper strips and serve hot. Makes 4 servings.

—— CREOLE GUMBO POT ——

1 small eggplant
2 teaspoons salt
3 tablespoons olive oil
1 large onion, chopped
1 red pepper, seeded, diced
1 clove garlic, crushed
2 teaspoons paprika
1/2 teaspoon hot chili powder
4 ounces fresh okra
3/4 cup frozen corn, thawed
2 cups boiling chicken stock
1 (8-oz.) can tomatoes in tomato juice
2 tablespoons long grain white rice
8 ounces peeled cooked medium-size
   shrimp, thawed if frozen
Salt and freshly ground pepper to taste
Fresh dill sprigs, if desired

Trim stalk end from eggplant. Cut in 1/2-inch pieces and place in a colander. Sprinkle with 2 teaspoons salt; let stand 30 minutes. Rinse under cold water and drain well.

Heat olive oil in a saucepan. Add eggplant, onion, red pepper and garlic and fry over low heat 5 minutes, stirring frequently. Stir in paprika and chili powder and cook gently 2 minutes.

Trim stalk ends from okra and discard. Cut okra in quarters.

Add okra, corn, chicken stock and tomatoes to eggplant mixture. Break up tomatoes with a spoon. Stir in rice, cover and simmer gently 25 minutes or until vegetables and rice are tender.

Add shrimp to mixture and heat through 5 minutes, stirring occasionally. Season with salt and pepper. Garnish with dill sprigs, if desired. Makes 4 to 6 servings.

Variation: Stir in 2/3 cup half and half and heat through just before serving.

DHAL

1-1/4 cups brown lentils
3-3/4 cups water
1 teaspoon turmeric
1 clove garlic, crushed
2 tablespoons ghee
1 large onion, chopped
1 teaspoon Garam Masala, page 12
1/2 teaspoon ground ginger
1 teaspoon coriander
1/2 teaspoon cayenne pepper
Fresh cilantro sprigs, if desired

Wash lentils in cold water.

In a saucepan, combine lentils, water, turmeric and garlic. Cover and simmer 30 minutes or until lentils are tender. Uncover and cook 2 to 3 minutes to reduce excess liquid.

Heat ghee in a saucepan. Add onion and fry gently 5 minutes. Add Garam Masala, ginger, coriander and cayenne pepper; cook gently 1 minute. Add mixture to lentils and stir well. Garnish with cilantro, if desired. Makes 4 to 6 servings.

NOTE: For a less fiery flavor, reduce cayenne pepper.

——— BARBECUED SPARERIBS ———

2 pounds pork spareribs
2 tablespoons dark soy sauce
1 tablespoon tomato paste
2 good pinches Five Spice Powder,
    page 12
3 tablespoons honey
1 clove garlic, crushed
1 (1/2-inch) piece ginger root, peeled,
    grated
1/2 cup unsweetened orange juice
1/4 teaspoon mustard powder
Orange peel, if desired

Preheat oven to 375F (190C). Cut ribs in single portions and arrange in a single layer in a roasting pan.

Mix remaining ingredients in a bowl until thoroughly combined. Spoon approximately 1/2 of sauce over ribs and bake in preheated oven 30 minutes.

Increase oven temperature to 400F (205C). Turn ribs and spoon remaining sauce over ribs. Bake 50 to 60 minutes, basting and turning frequently until ribs are glazed and rich golden brown. Garnish with orange peel, if desired, and serve hot. Makes 4 servings.

— FRIED DEVILED CAMEMBERT —

4 (1-1/2-oz.) pieces fairly firm
  Camembert cheese
2 teaspoons all-purpose flour
1/2 teaspoon dry mustard
1/2 teaspoon dried mixed herbs
Freshly ground pepper to taste
1 egg, beaten
1/4 cup dry bread crumbs
1/2 teaspoon hot chili powder
3 to 4 pinches cayenne pepper
Vegetable oil for deep frying
Fresh sage, rosemary and thyme
  sprigs, if desired

Wrap and freeze cheese 1 hour.

On a plate, combine flour, mustard, herbs
and pepper. Dredge each piece of cheese
thoroughly with mixture, then dip into
egg. In a small bowl, mix bread crumbs
with chili powder and cayenne pepper.
Coat dipped cheese portions in mixture,
pressing on firmly with palms of hands.

Half fill a deep-fat fryer or saucepan with
oil. Heat to 375F (190C) or until a 1/2-inch
cube of day-old bread browns in 40
seconds. Fry cheese about 30 seconds or
until golden brown. Drain on paper towels. Garnish with sage, rosemary and
thyme sprigs, if desired, and serve at once.
Makes 4 servings.

GUACAMOLE

2 ripe avocados
1 tablespoon lemon juice
1 small clove garlic, if desired
1 small fresh green chili, seeded
1 shallot, finely chopped
1 tablespoon olive oil
Few drops hot-pepper sauce
Salt to taste
1 lemon slice, cut in pieces
Fresh Italian parsley sprig, if desired
Tortilla chips

Cut avocados in half, remove seeds and scoop flesh onto a plate . Mash well.

Add lemon juice and garlic, if desired, and mix well. Very finely chop chili and add to mixture with shallot.

Stir in olive oil, hot-pepper sauce and salt and mix well. Spoon mixture into a serving bowl and garnish with lemon pieces and parsley sprig, if desired. Serve with tortilla chips. Makes 4 to 6 servings.

— EGG MAYONNAISE INDIENNE —

4 hard-boiled eggs
1 (3-1/2-oz.) can tuna, drained, flaked
1/2 cup mayonnaise
Salt and freshly ground pepper to taste
4 cocktail gherkins, chopped
3 tablespoons half and half
2 teaspoons tomato paste
1-1/2 teaspoons Curry Powder, page 12
Paprika
Fresh Italian parsley sprigs, if desired

Cut eggs in half lengthwise and carefully remove yolks.

Put yolks into a bowl. Mix in tuna, 2 table-spoons of mayonnaise, salt, pepper and gherkins. Divide mixture evenly between egg white halves and fill hollows. Smooth tops to form neat mounds.

In a bowl, mix remaining mayonnaise, half and half, tomato paste and Curry Powder; season with salt. Mix until smooth. Spoon mixture over prepared eggs to coat completely. Garnish with paprika and parsley sprigs, if desired. Serve chilled. Makes 4 servings.

DEVILED SMELT

12 ounces smelt, thawed if frozen
1/4 cup all-purpose flour
1/4 teaspoon salt
1 teaspoon dry mustard
1/4 teaspoon cayenne pepper
1/2 teaspoon paprika
Finely grated peel 1 lemon
Vegetable oil for deep frying
1 to 2 tablespoons chopped fresh
  parsley
Lemon wedges
Lemon peel strips, if desired
Fresh dill sprig, if desired

Rinse smelt under cold running water. Pat dry on paper towels.

In a plastic bag, combine flour, salt, mustard, cayenne pepper, paprika and lemon peel. Add smelt and shake well until fish are evenly coated. Half fill a deep-fat fryer or saucepan with oil; heat to 375F (190C) or until a 1/2-inch cube of day-old bread browns in 40 seconds.

Place 1/2 of smelt in a frying basket. Lower basket gradually into hot oil and fry 1 minute, shaking basket frequently. Drain on paper towels. Reheat oil to 375F (190C). Repeat with remaining smelt. Place all of smelt into basket and fry 1 to 2 minutes more or until lightly golden and crisp. Drain on paper towels. Turn into a warm serving dish, sprinkle with chopped parsley and serve hot with lemon wedges. Garnish with lemon peel strips and dill sprig, if desired. Makes 4 servings.

—— SESAME SHRIMP TOASTS ——

6 ounces cooked peeled medium-size
   shrimp, thawed if frozen
1 (3/4-inch) piece ginger root, peeled,
   grated
1 clove garlic, crushed
2 teaspoons cornstarch
1 egg white
3 pinches Five Spice Powder, page 12
Salt and freshly ground pepper to taste
4 thin slices white bread, crusts
   removed
3 tablespoons sesame seeds
Vegetable oil for shallow frying
Green onion daisies

Drain shrimp well on paper towels.

Mince shrimp finely. In a bowl, mix shrimp
with ginger, garlic and cornstarch. Lightly
whisk egg white with a fork (just enough to
make frothy) and add to shrimp. Stir in
Five Spice Powder, salt and pepper; mix
well.

Press shrimp mixture evenly and firmly
onto slices of bread. Sprinkle with sesame
seeds and press on firmly. Heat 3/4-inch oil
in a large skillet. Lower slices of bread,
shrimp-sides down, into hot oil and fry 2 to
3 minutes or until golden brown. Keep
slices immersed in oil. Drain on paper towels. Cut into fingers and garnish with
green onion daisies. Serve hot. Makes 4
servings.

MULLIGATAWNY SOUP

3 tablespoons butter
1 tablespoon corn oil
1 large onion, chopped
2 stalks celery, sliced thinly
3 carrots, diced
1-1/2 tablespoons Curry Powder,
    page 12
2 tablespoons all-purpose flour
5 cups chicken stock
2 tablespoons long grain white rice
2 tomatoes, peeled, chopped
8 ounces cooked chicken, diced
1 small cooking apple, peeled,
    cored, diced
Salt to taste
Fresh celery leaves, if desired
Carrot strip, if desired

Heat butter and oil in a saucepan.

Add onion, celery and carrots; cook gently
5 minutes. Stir in Curry Powder and flour
and cook 1 minute. Stir in stock and bring
to a boil; add rice and stir well.

Cover and simmer 20 minutes, stirring
occasionally. Add tomatoes, chicken,
apple and salt. Cover again and simmer 15
minutes. Garnish with celery leaves and
carrot strip, if desired, and serve hot.
Makes 4 servings.

BEEF SATAY

3 tablespoons corn oil
1 small onion, finely chopped
1 clove garlic, crushed
1/2 teaspoon hot chili powder
1 to 1-1/2 teaspoons Curry Powder,
  page 12
1-1/4 cups water
2/3 cup crunchy peanut butter
1 teaspoon light-brown sugar
2 teaspoons dark soy sauce
1 teaspoon lemon juice
Salt and freshly ground pepper to taste
1 pound boneless sirloin steak
Lemon pieces, if desired
Fresh cilantro sprigs, if desired

To make peanut sauce, heat 2 tablespoons of oil in a saucepan. Add onion and garlic and fry gently until golden.

Stir in chili powder, Curry Powder, water, peanut butter and brown sugar. Bring to a boil; simmer gently until thickened. Stir in soy sauce and lemon juice, then salt and pepper. Turn mixture into a serving dish.

Preheat broiler. Grease a broiler pan. Trim and cut meat in 1/2-inch cubes. Thread (not too tightly) onto 8 bamboo skewers, leaving a space at each end for holding. Cover ends with small pieces of foil to prevent burning. Place skewers in greased broiler pan. Brush with remaining 1 tablespoon oil. Cook under preheated broiler 10 to 15 minutes until golden and cooked through. Turn and brush frequently with oil during cooking. Garnish with lemon pieces and cilantro sprigs, if desired, and serve hot with peanut sauce. Makes 4 servings.

—— PIQUANT SALMON ROLLS ——

4 ounces cream cheese
1/4 cup walnuts, chopped
1 tablespoon chopped fresh chives
1 stalk celery, chopped
3 teaspoons lemon juice
Several pinches cayenne pepper
1/4 teaspoon ground coriander
8 (4" x 2") thin slices smoked salmon
8 thin slices whole-wheat bread
Butter
8 thin slices cucumber
Freshly ground pepper
Fresh dill sprigs, if desired
Chives, if desired

In a bowl, soften cream cheese and stir in walnuts, chives and celery.

Add 2 teaspoons of lemon juice and spices and mix well. Spread cream cheese mixture on each slice of salmon and season with pepper. Roll up to form neat rolls.

Toast slices of bread and cut 8 (2-1/2-inch) rounds, using a biscuit cutter. Spread thinly with butter. Place a cucumber slice on each bread round and place a salmon roll on top of each cucumber. Drizzle with remaining lemon juice and garnish with dill sprigs and chives, if desired. Makes 4 servings.

NOTE: Salmon rolls can be prepared several hours in advance and refrigerated. Toast bases, however, are better freshly made. Once assembled, serve within 30 minutes.

─── SPICY BEEF LETTUCE CUPS ───

12 ounces boneless sirloin steak,
  trimmed
2 tablespoons light soy sauce
1 tablespoon dry sherry
1 (1/2-inch) piece ginger root, peeled,
  grated
1 clove garlic, crushed
2 pinches Five Spice Powder, page 12
1 teaspoon chili sauce
2 tablespoons corn oil
6 green onions, sliced diagonally
1 small red bell pepper, seeded, diced
1/2 teaspoon cornstarch
1 teaspoon water
8 crisp lettuce cups, chilled
Fresh parsley sprigs, if desired

Cut steak in very thin slivers and place in a
bowl.

Add soy sauce, sherry, ginger, garlic, Five
Spice Powder and chili sauce; mix well.
Cover and refrigerate 1 hour, stirring occasionally. Heat oil in a skillet or wok. Add
onions and red pepper; stir-fry 1 minute.

Add beef mixture to onion mixture and
stir-fry 2 to 3 minutes. In a custard cup,
blend cornstarch and water until smooth;
add to beef mixture. Cook 1 minute, stirring constantly. Spoon beef mixture into
lettuce cups. Garnish with parsley sprigs,
if desired. Makes 4 servings.

—— CURRY CREAM MUSSELS ——

2 pounds mussels, cleaned, page 25
2/3 cup water
2/3 cup dry cider
3 sprigs fresh thyme
1 clove garlic, crushed
2 tablespoons butter
3 shallots, finely chopped
1 stalk celery, finely chopped
1 tablespoon Curry Powder, page 12
1 tablespoon all-purpose flour
1/4 cup half and half
1/4 cup mayonnaise
Fresh dill sprigs, if desired
Hot crusty bread

Place cleaned mussels in a saucepan with water, cider, thyme and garlic. Cover and cook over high heat, shaking pan frequently, 6 to 7 minutes or until shells open. Discard any mussels which remain closed. Cool mussels in liquid. Drain off cooled liquid, strain through a fine sieve and reserve. Discard thyme. Remove a half shell from each mussel and arrange mussels on 4 serving plates.

Melt butter in a saucepan. Add shallots and celery and cook gently 5 minutes. Add Curry Powder and flour and cook 1 minute. Stir in 1 cup of reserved liquid. Bring to a boil, stirring constantly. Cover and cook gently 10 minutes, stirring frequently. Cool. Stir in half and half and mayonnaise and mix well. Spoon sauce over mussels and garnish with dill sprigs, if desired. Serve with bread. Makes 4 servings.

GADO GADO

8 ounces white cabbage
1/4 cup sesame oil
1 large onion, cut in fourths, thinly
   sliced
1 green bell pepper, seeded, thinly
   sliced
6 ounces fresh bean sprouts
1 fresh green chili, seeded, finely
   chopped
1 clove garlic, crushed
2 shallots, finely chopped
1/2 teaspoon ground cumin
1/3 cup smooth peanut butter
3 tablespoons lemon juice
Few drops hot-pepper sauce
1/3 cup water
Red bell pepper strips, if desired

Finely shred cabbage, discarding stalk.

Heat 2 tablespoons of sesame oil in a skillet. Add cabbage, onion, thinly sliced bell pepper, bean sprouts and chili and fry over fairly high heat 3 to 4 minutes, stirring constantly. Remove from heat, spoon mixture into a serving dish; cool.

To make sauce, heat remaining sesame oil in saucepan. Add garlic, shallots and cumin and fry gently 5 minutes. Add peanut butter and cook gently 2 minutes. Stir in lemon juice, hot-pepper sauce and water and heat through gently to form a fairly thick sauce. Garnish sauce with bell pepper strips, if desired, and serve with cooled vegetables. Makes 4 to 6 servings.

— PEPPERED FARMHOUSE PÂTÉ —

8 slices bacon
1 pound fresh pork picnic shoulder
12 ounces pork liver
1 onion, quartered
1 clove garlic
8 ounces veal cutlets
1 egg, beaten
1 teaspoon salt
2 teaspoons green peppercorns
1 teaspoon dried mixed herbs
2 tablespoons brandy
Additional green peppercorns, if
   desired
Fresh bay leaf, if desired
Crusty bread

Preheat oven to 350F (175C). Remove rinds and bones from bacon and pork.

Stretch bacon on a board using back of a knife until bacon is almost double in length. Line bottom and sides of a 5-cup terrine or soufflé dish with bacon. Mince shoulder pork, liver, onion and garlic. Cut veal in 1/2-inch pieces. In a bowl, combine pork shoulder, liver, veal, onion and garlic. Stir in egg, salt, peppercorns, herbs and brandy; mix thoroughly.

Spoon mixture into bacon-lined dish and smooth surface. Cover tightly with foil. Put into a roasting pan half filled with hot water. Bake in preheated oven 2 hours. Cool 30 minutes. Top with a plate and place a heavy weight on plate. Cool completely, then refrigerate overnight. Turn out onto a serving plate. Garnish with additional green peppercorns and bay leaf, if desired, and serve with bread. Makes 8 servings.

— ORANGE GINGER DUCKLING —

1 (4 lb.) oven-ready duckling
3 tablespoons corn oil
8 ounces Chinese pea pods, ends
   removed
3 stalks celery, sliced diagonally
12 green onions, sliced diagonally
1 red pepper, seeded, cut in small
   diamonds
1 (3-inch) piece ginger root, peeled,
   chopped
1 tablespoon granulated sugar
1 tablespoon soy sauce
1 tablespoon dry sherry
1 tablespoon malt vinegar
1 tablespoon tomato paste
2 teaspoons cornstarch
2/3 cup orange juice

Preheat oven to 350F (175C). Prick duckling skin all over with a fork and put into a roasting pan. Bake in preheated oven 1-3/4 hours until golden and cooked; cool. Strip flesh and skin from carcass and cut in thin strips. Heat 2 tablespoons of oil in a large skillet or wok. Add pea pods and celery and stir-fry 2 minutes. Add green onions, red pepper and ginger and stir-fry 2 minutes. Remove from skillet and keep warm.

Heat remaining oil in skillet. Add duckling; stir-fry 2 minutes. Remove from skillet; keep warm. In a small bowl, mix sugar, soy sauce, sherry, vinegar and tomato paste. Blend cornstarch with a little orange juice, then stir in remaining juice. Add to soy sauce mixture. Pour into skillet; bring to a boil, stirring constantly. Reduce heat; simmer 2 minutes. Add vegetables and duckling to sauce and heat through. Makes 4 servings.

NOTE: Serve with rice, garnished with orange pieces and Chinese snow peas, noodles and crisp shrimp crackers.

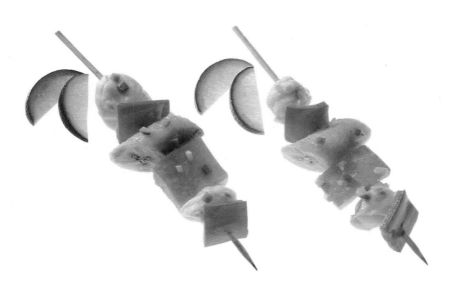

—— TROPICAL FISH KEBABS ——

2 pounds monkfish
2 cloves garlic, crushed
1 fresh green chili, seeded, chopped
1 (1-inch) piece ginger root, peeled,
    chopped
Juice 1 lime
Salt and freshly ground pepper to taste
1/3 cup corn oil
1 ripe mango
2 bananas
1 red bell pepper, seeded, cut in cubes
Lime wedges

Cut away monkfish from central bone. Cut flesh in bite-size pieces.

In a shallow glass dish, combine garlic, chili, ginger, lime juice, salt, pepper and oil. Add fish and stir gently. Cover and refrigerate 2 hours. Meanwhile, slice mango lengthwise on each side, close to seed. Peel and cut mango flesh in small pieces. Preheat grill. Cut bananas in chunky pieces.

On 4 long or 8 short bamboo skewers, alternate fish with cubes of bell pepper, mango and banana. Arrange skewers in a broiler pan and spoon marinade over skewers. Broil 12 to 15 minutes, turning frequently and basting with marinade, or until cooked through. Serve with lime wedges. Makes 4 servings.

Variation: Substitute fresh pineapple for mango.

── SPICED CHICKEN PILAU ──

1/4 cup ghee
2 large onions, cut in thin slices
4 (4-oz.) skinned boneless chicken
   breasts, cubed
1/2 teaspoon turmeric
2 cups basmati rice
3-3/4 cups boiling chicken stock
5 green cardamom pods, crushed,
   seeds removed
1/2 teaspoon ground cinnamon
4 whole cloves
1/2 teaspoon fenugreek
1 teaspoon salt
3/4 cup frozen green peas, thawed
1/2 cup unsalted cashews
1/2 cup golden raisins
Green onion daisy, if desired
Red bell pepper strips, if desired
Fresh parsley sprig, if desired

Melt ghee in a large saucepan. Add onions
and chicken and fry 3 minutes, stirring
constantly. Add turmeric and rice; cook 2
minutes, stirring constantly. Stir in stock,
cardamom seeds, cinnamon, cloves,
fenugreek and salt. Bring to a boil. Stir
well, cover and cook gently 20 minutes.

Add green peas, cashews and raisins. Fluff
mixture with a fork, cover and cook 10
minutes. Fluff again with a fork. Garnish
with green onion daisy, bell pepper strips
and parsley sprig, if desired, and serve
hot. Makes 6 servings.

—— PEPPERED SALAMI SALAD ——

1/2 cup olive oil
2 cloves garlic, crushed
3 slices white bread, crusts removed,
  cubed
1/2 teaspoon chili seasoning
8 ounces young spinach or 1 cos
  lettuce
1 (6-oz.) piece peppered salami, diced
3 small onions, sliced, separated in
  rings
1 red bell pepper, seeded, cut in thin
  strips
4 ounces button mushrooms, sliced
1-1/2 tablespoons lemon juice
1 teaspoon sugar
1 teaspoon prepared mustard
Salt and freshly ground pepper to taste
12 Marinated Spiced Olives, page 14

Heat 3 tablespoons of oil in a skillet. Add garlic and bread cubes and fry, stirring constantly, until golden. Remove from heat. Add chili seasoning, stir well and cool. Tear spinach or lettuce leaves in bite-size pieces. In a large salad bowl, combine spinach or lettuce leaves, salami, onion, bell pepper and mushrooms.

Place remaining oil in a screw-top jar with lemon juice, sugar, mustard, salt and pepper. Shake vigorously until well blended. Pour over salad and toss well. Sprinkle croutons on top and garnish with olives. Serve at once. Makes 4 servings.

NOTE: Salad (without dressing) may be prepared in advance and kept covered in refrigerator. Just before serving, shake dressing ingredients vigorously, add to salad and toss well. Add croutons and olives and serve at once.

SINGAPORE CURRY PUFFS

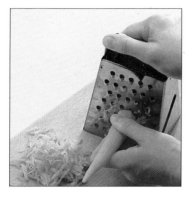

1 cup all-purpose flour
1 egg
2/3 cup milk
2/3 cup cold water
About 5 tablespoons corn oil
1 onion, chopped
8 ounces lean ground beef
2 carrots, grated
1 parsnip, grated
2 teaspoons Curry Powder, page 12
1 tablespoon tomato paste
2 teaspoons cornstarch
2/3 cup beef stock
1 egg, beaten
Vegetable oil for deep frying
Carrot strip, if desired

Sift flour into a bowl. Make a well in center and add egg. Gradually stir in milk and beat well until smooth. Stir in cold water and beat well. Pour batter into a pitcher.

Heat a little oil in a small skillet and pour off excess. Pour a little batter into skillet, swirling skillet to spread batter evenly over bottom to make a thin coating. Cook until underside is golden, then turn pancake out of pan (do not cook other side). Repeat with remaining batter, adding more oil to pan each time, to make 8 pancakes.

Heat 2 tablespoons oil in a saucepan. Add onion, ground beef, carrots, parsnip and curry powder. Cook gently 5 minutes, stirring constantly. Add tomato paste and mix well. Blend cornstarch with a little stock. Add remaining stock to ground beef mixture and bring to a boil. Add cornstarch mixture and cook 2 minutes, stirring constantly. Simmer mixture 10 minutes.

Lay pancakes, cooked-sides up, on a flat surface. Spread filling in a 2-inch-horizontal line across center to within 1-1/2 inches of side edges. Fold these side edges over mixture and then fold remaining top and bottom edges over to cover filling. Brush with egg and fold pancakes in half. Chill 1 hour.

Half fill a deep fat fryer or saucepan with oil; heat to 350F (175C) or until a 1/2-inch bread cube browns in 40 seconds. Fry folded pancakes, 4 at a time, 2 to 3 minutes or until golden brown and heated through. Drain on paper towels. Garnish with carrot strip, if desired, and serve hot. Makes 8 servings.

DEVILED CRAB QUICHE

2 cups all-purpose flour
1/2 teaspoon salt
1/2 teaspoon chili seasoning
1/4 cup cold margarine, diced
1/4 cup lard, diced
1/2 cup (2 oz.) finely grated Cheddar
  cheese
3 tablespoons cold water
6 slices bacon, chopped
1 onion, chopped
4 ounces crabmeat, flaked
3 eggs
2/3 cup half and half
1/2 teaspoon mustard powder
1/4 teaspoon cayenne pepper
Salt to taste
Tomato slices, if desired
Fresh Italian parsley sprigs, if desired

Preheat oven to 400F (205C). In a bowl, combine flour, salt and chili seasoning. Cut in margarine and lard until mixture resembles bread crumbs. Add cheese and mix well. Stir in cold water and mix to form a fairly firm dough. Knead gently on a floured surface and roll out pastry. Set a 10-inch fluted flan pan with a removable bottom on a baking sheet. Press pastry into flutes and trim edge neatly. Prick base with a fork. Line pastry with waxed paper and fill with dried beans.

Bake 15 minutes. Remove waxed paper and beans and bake 5 to 10 minutes more or until dry and lightly golden. Fry bacon 3 minutes. Add onion; cook 2 minutes. Remove from heat; mix with crabmeat. Spoon mixture into flan shell. Whisk eggs, half and half, mustard, cayenne and salt. Pour into flan shell. Bake 30 to 35 minutes or until set and lightly golden. Garnish with tomato and parsley, if desired, and serve warm or cold. Makes 6 to 8 servings.

− MUSTARD MOZZARELLA PORK −

1 tablespoon butter
1 tablespoon oil
4 (6-oz.) pork steaks
1 onion, finely chopped
1 clove garlic, crushed
1 tablespoon Dijon-style mustard
1/4 cup dry white wine
3 tablespoons half and half
Salt and freshly ground pepper to taste
1-1/4 cups chopped Mozzarella cheese
Lemon wedges, if desired
Cucumber slices, if desired
Sliced celery, if desired
Fresh watercress sprigs, if desired

Heat butter and oil in a skillet. Add pork steaks and fry quickly 3 minutes on each side.

Cover and cook gently 15 minutes, turning occasionally. Remove pork steaks to a shallow flameproof dish; keep warm. Add onion and garlic to skillet and cook 5 minutes.

Add mustard and wine to onion mixture. Stir well, then bring to a boil. Boil 1-1/2 minutes. Stir in half and half and heat through gently. Season with salt and pepper. Spoon mixture over pork steaks and sprinkle with cheese. Preheat broiler. Broil 5 minutes or until cheese is melted and bubbling. Serve hot with lemon wedges, cucumber slices, celery and watercress sprigs, if desired. Makes 4 servings.

CHILI BEAN TACOS

2 tablespoons olive oil
1 pound pork sausage, crumbled
1 onion, chopped
1 clove garlic, crushed
1/2 teaspoon ground cumin
1 teaspoon hot chili powder
1 tomato, peeled, chopped
3 tablespoons tomato paste
1/2 red bell pepper, seeded, diced
1 (10-oz.) can kidney beans, drained
Salt to taste
8 taco shells
Sour cream
Paprika
Lettuce leaves
Radish roses

Preheat oven to 350F (175C). Heat oil in a saucepan. Add sausage, onion, garlic, cumin and chili powder; fry gently 5 minutes, stirring to break up sausage. Add tomato, tomato paste, bell pepper and kidney beans. Stir well and cook gently 15 minutes, stirring frequently to prevent mixture sticking. Season with salt.

Meanwhile, heat taco shells following package instructions. Fill hot taco shells with sausage mixture. Top each taco with sour cream and sprinkle with paprika. Serve with lettuce leaves and radish roses. Makes 8 tacos.

Variation: Substitute lean ground beef for sausage, if desired.

— SCANDINAVIAN FISH SALAD —

2/3 cup malt vinegar
2/3 cup water
3 tablespoons sugar
1 tablespoon Pickling Spice, page 13
4 fresh herrings, cleaned, filleted
1-1/4 cups sour cream
3 tablespoons mayonnaise
2 teaspoons Dijon-style mustard
1 onion, halved, thinly sliced
1 green delicious apple
1 red delicious apple
Red leaf lettuce leaves, if desired
4 green onion daisies, if desired
Fresh dill sprigs, if desired

In a small saucepan, combine vinegar and water. Add sugar and Pickling Spice.

Bring to a boil, stirring to dissolve sugar. Boil 2 minutes; cool. Strain and discard spices. Cut herring fillets in 1/2-inch-wide strips and place in a shallow dish. Pour cold marinade over fish. Cover and marinate several hours or overnight.

Drain herring strips. In a bowl, combine sour cream, mayonnaise, mustard and onion. Cut apples in fourths, remove cores and slice thinly (do not peel). Add sliced apples and herrings to sour cream mixture and mix together gently until coated with dressing. Arrange lettuce leaves on 4 plates. Spoon herring mixture on plates and garnish with green onion daisies and dill sprigs, if desired. Serve chilled. Makes 4 servings.

— TANGY GLAZED DRUMSTICKS —

1 small onion, chopped
1 tablespoon honey
1 clove garlic, crushed
3 tablespoons corn oil
3 tablespoons catsup
1 tablespoon tomato paste
2 teaspoons Worcestershire sauce
1 teaspoon chili sauce
2 pinches Five Spice Powder, page 12
8 chicken drumsticks
Fresh watercress sprigs, if desired
Lemon slices, if desired

In a saucepan, combine onion, honey, garlic, 2 tablespoons of oil, catsup and tomato paste.

Add Worcestershire sauce, chili sauce and Five Spice Powder and simmer, uncovered, 5 minutes, stirring occasionally. In a blender or food processor, process mixture to a smooth purée. Add remaining oil and stir well.

Arrange chicken in a roasting pan. Brush with marinade and let stand 1 hour. Meanwhile, preheat oven to 400F (205C). Bake chicken in preheated oven 35 to 40 minutes, turning and brushing frequently with marinade juices. Serve hot or cold, garnished with watercress sprigs and lemon slices, if desired.

Makes 4 servings.

── STIR-FRY PORK & PEPPERS ──

3 pinches Five Spice Powder, page 12
2 tablespoons dry sherry or sake
2 tablespoons light soy sauce
1 clove garlic, crushed
1 (1-inch) piece ginger root, peeled,
   chopped
1 pound pork tenderloin, cut in thin
   strips
2 onions
1/4 cup corn oil
1 red bell pepper, seeded, cut in
   thin strips
1 green bell pepper, seeded, cut in
   thin strips
3 ounces button mushrooms, sliced
6 canned whole water chestnuts, sliced
2 teaspoons cornstarch
2/3 cup chicken stock
Leek curls, if desired
Green onion curls, if desired

In a bowl, combine Five Spice Powder, sherry, soy sauce, garlic and ginger. Add pork, stir well and let stand 30 minutes. Cut onions in eighths and separate in layers. Heat 2 tablespoons of oil in a skillet or wok. Drain pork, reserve marinade. Add pork to oil and stir-fry 5 minutes. Remove from skillet and keep warm.

Add remaining oil to skillet. Add onions, bell peppers, mushrooms and water chestnuts. Stir-fry 3 minutes. Add vegetable mixture to pork. Blend cornstarch with reserved marinade and 2 tablespoons of stock. Add remaining stock to skillet and bring to a boil. Add cornstarch mixture and cook 2 minutes, stirring constantly. Add pork and vegetables to stock and heat through, stirring constantly. Garnish with leek and green onion curls, if desired, and serve hot. Makes 4 servings.

— CLAM & SHRIMP CHOWDER —

1/4 cup butter
1 large onion, chopped
2 stalks celery, chopped
2 potatoes, peeled, diced
1-1/2 teaspoons fennel seeds
2 tablespoons all-purpose flour
1 teaspoon paprika
1-3/4 cups chicken stock
1 (10-oz.) can baby clams, drained
4 ounces cooked peeled medium-size
   shrimp, thawed if frozen
1 red bell pepper, seeded, diced
3/4 cup frozen corn, thawed
2/3 cup half and half
Salt and freshly ground pepper to taste
Fresh dill sprig, if desired

Melt butter in a saucepan. Add onion, celery, potatoes and fennel. Cook gently 5 minutes, stirring frequently. Blend in flour and cook 1 minute. Stir in paprika and stock and bring to a boil, stirring constantly.

Cover, reduce heat and simmer 15 minutes, stirring occasionally. Stir in clams, shrimp, bell pepper and corn. Simmer 5 minutes. Stir in half and half, salt and pepper. Garnish with dill sprig, if desired, and serve hot. Makes 4 servings.

Variation: Omit paprika and add 1 teaspoon Curry Powder, page 12. Add 1 tablespoon chopped fresh parsley or cilantro just before serving.

─── CREOLE JAMBALAYA ───

2 tablespoons olive oil
8 ounces ham, diced
8 ounces chorizo sausage, sliced
1 large Spanish onion, chopped
3 cloves garlic, crushed
1/2 teaspoon dried thyme
2 tablespoons chopped fresh parsley
1-1/2 cups boiling chicken stock
1-1/2 cups long grain white rice
1/4 teaspoon cayenne pepper
1 teaspoon hot-pepper sauce
1 (14-oz.) can tomatoes
1 green bell pepper, seeded, diced
2 tablespoons dry white wine
Tomato slices, if desired
Fresh thyme sprigs, if desired

Heat oil in a saucepan. Add ham, sausage and onion. Fry gently 3 minutes. Add garlic, thyme and parsley. Stir well, then add stock, rice, cayenne and hot-pepper sauce; mix well. Add tomatoes with juice and break up with a spoon. Bring mixture to a boil, stir well, then cover and simmer gently 15 minutes.

Stir in bell pepper and wine. Cover and cook 8 minutes or until liquid is absorbed. Fluff with a fork. Garnish with tomato slices and thyme sprigs, if desired, and serve hot. Makes 4 to 6 servings.

Variation: Add 4 ounces cooked peeled medium-size shrimp, thawed, if frozen, to mixture 5 minutes before end of cooking time. For a fierier flavor, add more cayenne and hot-pepper sauce to taste.

STEAK AU POIVRE

1-1/2 teaspoons green peppercorns
1 teaspoon black peppercorns
1 teaspoon white peppercorns
4 (6-oz.) boneless strip beef steaks
3 tablespoons unsalted butter
Few drops hot-pepper sauce
Few drops Worcestershire sauce
2 tablespoons brandy
3 tablespoons whipping cream
Salt to taste

Coarsely crush all peppercorns in a pestle and mortar.

Sprinkle crushed pepper over both sides of steaks, pressing in well with palm of hand. Let stand 30 minutes. Melt 1 tablespoon of butter in a skillet and heat until foaming. Add steaks and cook 2 to 3 minutes, then turn and cook other sides 2 to 3 minutes. (This timing gives medium-rare steaks, so adjust cooking time to suit personal preference.)

Turn steaks again and top each one with remaining butter and sprinkle with a few drops hot-pepper sauce and Worcestershire sauce. Pour brandy over steaks and allow to heat through a few seconds. Flame and remove from heat. When flames subside, remove steaks to a warm serving plate and keep warm. Add whipping cream to skillet and stir well. Heat through 1 minute, scraping up sediment from bottom of skillet. Season with salt and spoon mixture over steaks. Serve at once. Makes 4 servings.

NOTE: Serve with fried potatoes and a green salad. Garnish with a fresh Italian parsley sprig, if desired.

CHILI-CHEESE BURGERS

2 tablespoons olive oil
2 onions, finely chopped
2 cloves garlic, crushed
1 (8-oz.) can tomatoes in tomato juice
1 (3-1/2-oz.) can green chilies
1 tablespoon chili relish
1/2 teaspoon cumin seeds
1 pound lean ground beef
Salt and freshly ground pepper to taste
2 tablespoons corn oil
4 slices Gruyère cheese
Shredded lettuce
4 buns, split, warmed
Onion slices

Heat olive oil in a saucepan. Add 1 chopped onion and garlic and fry gently 5 minutes. Process tomatoes in a blender or food processor to a purée. Drain and chop chilies. Add tomatoes, chilies, chili relish and cumin to onion mixture. Stir well, then cover and simmer 10 minutes, stirring occasionally.

Meanwhile, put ground beef into a bowl. Add remaining onion, salt and pepper; mix well. Divide into 4 equal balls and shape each in a 4-1/2-inch round burger. Heat corn oil in a large skillet. Add burgers and fry 5 to 6 minutes on each side. Top each with a slice of cheese. Arrange lettuce on 4 bun halves. Place burger on lettuce and top with chili sauce, onion and remaining bun halves. Serve hot in napkins. Makes 4 servings.

—— VEGETABLE COUSCOUS ——

8 ounces couscous
2 cups water
1/4 cup olive oil
2 onions, coarsely chopped
1 large eggplant, diced
1 (1 lb.) acorn squash, seeded, diced
2 carrots, sliced
1 teaspoon Harissa, page 13
2 tomatoes, peeled, chopped
2 tablespoons tomato paste
2 cups vegetable stock
1 (13-oz.) can garbanzo beans, drained
2 zucchini, sliced
1/3 cup raisins
2 tablespoons chopped fresh parsley
Fresh cilantro sprig, if desired

Combine couscous and water in a bowl. Let soak 15 minutes or until water is absorbed. Heat oil in a saucepan. Add onions, eggplant, squash and carrots and fry 5 minutes, stirring frequently. Stir in Harissa, tomatoes, tomato paste and stock. Bring to a boil and stir well.

Line a large metal sieve or colander with muslin or all-purpose kitchen cloth and place over pan. Spoon couscous into sieve. Cover pan with foil to enclose steam and simmer 20 minutes. Remove sieve. Add garbanzo beans, zucchini and raisins to vegetable mixture. Stir well, then replace sieve and fluff couscous with a fork. Cover again with foil and simmer 20 minutes. Spoon couscous on a large serving dish and fluff with a fork. Add parsley to vegetable mixture and spoon over couscous. Garnish with cilantro sprig, if desired, and serve hot. Makes 4 to 6 servings.

CURRIED SCALLOPS
IN CREAM SAUCE

8 large fresh scallops
1-1/4 cups water
1 slice lemon
1/2 bay leaf
1-1/2 pounds potatoes, cut in pieces
5 tablespoons butter
Salt and freshly ground pepper to taste
3 ounces button mushrooms, sliced
2 shallots, finely chopped
1/2 to 1 teaspoon Curry Powder,
   page 12
1/4 cup all-purpose flour
3 tablespoons whipping cream
2 tablespoons chopped fresh parsley
Fresh bay leaves, if desired
Lemon and lime twists, if desired
Fresh dill sprigs, if desired

Wash scallops, remove roe. Pat scallops dry and cut in slices.

Put scallops, water, lemon slice and bay leaf in a saucepan . Simmer gently 20 minutes. Strain, reserving liquid. Discard lemon and bay leaf. If necessary, add enough water to reserved liquid to make 1-1/4 cups liquid. Cook potatoes in boiling, salted water until tender. Drain and return to pan. Mash with 1 tablespoon of butter. Season with salt and pepper. Beat well; cool slightly. Transfer to a large pastry bag.

Preheat broiler. Pipe potato around edges of 4 ceramic scallop dishes. Melt remaining butter in a saucepan. Add mushrooms, shallots and Curry Powder and cook 2 minutes. Stir in flour and cook 1 minute. Add reserved liquid and bring to a boil. Reduce heat and simmer 2 minutes, stirring constantly. Remove from heat and stir in scallops, cream, parsley, salt and pepper. Spoon into dishes. Broil 4 to 5 minutes or until lightly golden. Garnish with bay leaves, citrus twists and dill sprigs, if desired, and serve hot. Makes 4 servings.

CHILI CON CARNE

2 tablespoons olive oil
1-1/2 pounds lean ground beef
2 onions, chopped
1 clove garlic, crushed
2 stalks celery, chopped
2 teaspoons hot chili powder
1 teaspoon cumin seeds
1 (14-oz.) can tomatoes
2 tablespoons tomato paste
1 (15-oz.) can red kidney beans,
    drained
Salt to taste
Steamed rice
Sour cream
Diced avocado
Onion slices
Fresh Italian parsley sprig, if desired

Preheat oven to 350F (175C). Heat oil in a flameproof casserole dish. Add ground beef, onions, garlic and celery and fry gently 5 minutes, stirring occasionally.

Add chili powder and cumin and cook gently 2 minutes. Add tomatoes and break up with a spoon. Stir in tomato paste and kidney beans. Bring to a boil, stirring frequently.

Cover and bake in preheated oven 1 hour, stirring occasionally. Season mixture with salt. Spoon chili over individual bowls of rice and top each serving with sour cream, avocado and onion. Garnish with parsley sprig, if desired. Makes 4 servings.

NOTE: For a fierier flavor, increase chili powder to 1 tablespoon. To prevent avocado discoloring, toss in lemon juice.

NASI GORENG

1-1/2 cups long grain white rice
3 tablespoons corn oil
2 onions, cut in half, sliced
2 cloves garlic, crushed
2 small fresh green chilies, seeded,
  chopped
1 (6-oz.) pork tenderloin, diced
1 (6-oz.) skinned chicken breast
1/4 teaspoon hot chili powder
1 teaspoon paprika
2 tablespoons light soy sauce
4 ounces cooked peeled medium-size
  shrimp, thawed if frozen
Salt to taste
1 egg
1 teaspoon cold water
1-1/2 teaspoons butter
Shrimp crackers

Cook rice in boiling, salted water 12 minutes. Drain and rinse well, then drain again. Heat oil in a large skillet. Add onions, garlic and chilies and fry 2 minutes. Add pork and chicken and fry gently 10 minutes until cooked. Add rice, chili powder, paprika, soy sauce and shrimp and cook 5 to 6 minutes or until piping hot, stirring constantly. Season with salt.

Turn mixture into a warm serving dish and keep warm while preparing omelette topping. Whisk egg with cold water. Melt butter in a skillet. Add egg mixture and swirl skillet to give a thin, even mixture. Cook over gentle heat 2 to 3 minutes or until egg mixture is set and lightly golden underneath. Turn omelette out onto a flat surface. Roll up and cut in slices. Arrange slices of omelette on top of rice mixture. Serve hot with shrimp crackers. Makes 4 servings.

INDIAN CHICKEN PIES

2 tablespoons butter
2 ounces button mushrooms, chopped
1 onion, chopped
2 teaspoons Garam Masala, page 12
3-1/4 cups all-purpose flour
2/3 cup chicken stock
8 ounces cooked chicken, diced
1/3 cup frozen corn, thawed
Salt and freshly ground pepper to taste
1/4 teaspoon salt
1/3 cup cold margarine, diced
1/3 cup lard, diced
1/4 cup cold water
1 egg, beaten
Tomato slices, if desired, cut in half
Fresh parsley sprigs, if desired

Melt butter in a saucepan. Add mushrooms, onion and Garam Masala and cook 2 minutes.

Stir in 1/4 cup of flour and cook 1 minute, then stir in stock and bring to a boil, stirring constantly. Reduce heat and cook 2 minutes, stirring constantly. Remove from heat and stir in chicken, corn, salt and pepper; cool.

Sift remaining flour into a bowl. Add 1/4 teaspoon salt and cut in margarine and lard finely until mixture resembles bread crumbs. Add cold water and mix to form a fairly firm dough. Knead gently until smooth.

Preheat oven to 375F (175C). Preheat a baking sheet. Cut off 2/3 of pastry and cut in 4 equal pieces. Roll each piece to a 7-inch circle. Line 4 (5-inch) fluted pan pans with removable bottoms with pastry circles, allowing pastry to overlap top edges slightly. Press pastry well into flutes but do not trim top edge. Cut remaining 1/3 of pastry in 4 equal pieces and roll each piece to a 6-inch circle.

Spoon cold chicken mixture into pastry-lined flan pans and smooth surfaces. Dampen edges of pastry in pans and cover with pastry circles. Seal edges well and trim by pressing pastry edges firmly with flat blade of a knife. Make a small hole in center of each pie. Reroll pastry trimmings and cut out leaves to decorate pies. Brush surfaces of pies with egg, then decorate with leaves and brush leaves with egg.

Place flan pans on preheated baking sheet and bake in preheated oven 40 to 45 minutes or until pastry is golden brown and filling is heated through. Cool before carefully removing from pans. Garnish with tomato slices and parsley sprigs, if desired, and serve cold. Makes 4.

Variation: Substitute Curry Powder, page 12 for Garam Masala or try a mixture of each.

— LAMB & MUSHROOM KORMA —

3 tablespoons corn oil
1 large onion, coarsely chopped
1 (1-1/2-inch) piece ginger root, peeled,
   chopped
2 cloves garlic, crushed
1 teaspoon ground cumin
1 teaspoon ground coriander
4 cardamom pods, crushed, seeded
1/2 teaspoon turmeric
1-1/2 pounds lean lamb, cut in cubes
1-1/4 cups plain yogurt
6 ounces button mushrooms, sliced
1 tablespoon lemon juice
Salt and freshly ground pepper to taste
Lime slices, if desired, cut in fourths
Fresh cilantro sprigs, if desired
Nan bread
Saffron rice

Heat oil in a saucepan. Add onion and fry gently until lightly golden. Add ginger, garlic, cumin, coriander, cardamom seeds and turmeric and fry gently 2 minutes, stirring constantly. Add lamb and fry until brown, stirring frequently. Stir in yogurt and bring to a boil.

Stir well, cover and cook gently 45 minutes, stirring occasionally. Add mushrooms, re-cover and cook 15 minutes or until lamb is tender and yogurt is absorbed. Stir in lemon juice, salt and pepper and cook, uncovered, 5 minutes. Garnish with lime pieces and cilantro sprigs, if desired, and serve hot with Nan bread and saffron rice. Makes 4 servings.

CHILI PEPPER PIZZA

3 tablespoons olive oil
1 onion, cut in fourths, sliced
1 clove garlic, crushed
1 (8-oz.) can tomatoes
1 tablespoon tomato paste
1/2 teaspoon dried oregano
1 cup all-purpose flour
1 cup whole-wheat flour
1/4 teaspoon salt
1 teaspoon active dried yeast
2/3 cup warm water
   (120F-130F/50C-55C)
1 (3-1/2-oz.) can green chilies
6 ounces Mozzarella cheese, chopped
2 ounces pepperoni or salami stick,
   sliced
8 ripe or green olives
Tomato roses, if desired
Fresh parsley sprigs, if desired

Lightly grease a 10-inch pizza pan. Heat 2 tablespoons of oil in a saucepan. Add onion, garlic, tomato paste, tomatoes with juice and oregano. Stir well to break up tomatoes, then simmer, uncovered, 10 to 15 minutes or until well thickened; cool. Preheat oven to 375F (190C). Put flours, salt and yeast in a bowl and mix well. Add water and mix to form a dough. Knead well, then roll to a 10-inch circle. Line greased pizza pan with dough.

Brush surface of dough with a little of remaining oil and cover with tomato mixture. Drain and chop chilies and sprinkle on top. Sprinkle with cheese and drizzle with remaining oil. Bake in preheated oven 25 minutes. Top pizza with pepperoni or salami and olives and bake 10 minutes. Cut in wedges. Garnish with tomato roses and parsley sprigs, if desired, and serve hot. Makes 2 to 4 servings.

— INDONESIAN COCONUT BEEF —

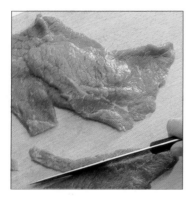

1-1/2 pounds boneless sirloin steak,
  trimmed
3 tablespoons corn oil
1 large Spanish onion, sliced
1 clove garlic, crushed
1 teaspoon ground ginger
1 teaspoon ground cumin
1 teaspoon ground coriander
1 teaspoon chili seasoning
2/3 cup shredded coconut
2 teaspoons light-brown sugar
1 tablespoon lemon juice
1-1/4 cups beef stock
Thin slivers red bell pepper
Chopped green chilies
Small slices onion

Cut steak in 1/2-inch thick strips.

Heat oil in a saucepan. Add Spanish onion
slices and garlic and fry gently until soft.
Add beef and fry, stirring, until brown.

Add spices to beef and cook 2 minutes.
Add coconut, brown sugar, lemon juice
and beef stock; stir well. Simmer gently,
uncovered, 30 to 35 minutes, stirring occasionally, or until mixture is thickened and
dry. Stir mixture more frequently towards
end of cooking time to prevent sticking.
Garnish with slivers of bell pepper, green
chilies and small slices onion. Makes 4
servings.

NOTE: If you prefer a more moist mixture,
cook 20 to 25 minutes instead of 30 to 35
minutes.

— CHEESY SPANISH OMELETTE —

1 tablespoon olive oil
2 tablespoons butter
1 onion, chopped
1 clove garlic, crushed
1 red bell pepper, seeded, diced
3/4 cup finely shredded green cabbage
4 slices bacon, chopped
1 teaspoon fenugreek
1/2 teaspoon ground coriander
4 eggs, beaten
1 tablespoon cold water
Salt and freshly ground pepper to taste
1/2 cup (1-1/2 oz.) grated Cheddar
    cheese
Red bell pepper strips, if desired
Fresh Italian parsley sprigs, if desired

Heat oil and butter in a medium-size flameproof skillet. Add onion, garlic, bell pepper, cabbage and bacon and fry over low heat 5 minutes, stirring occasionally. Add fenugreek and coriander and stir well.

Preheat broiler. Whisk eggs with cold water, salt and pepper and pour into skillet. Swirl skillet to ensure an even coating. Cook over low heat 3 to 4 minutes or until mixture is golden brown underneath. Sprinkle with cheese and place under preheated broiler and cook until mixture is set on top and cheese has melted. Cut in 4 wedges, garnish with bell pepper strips and parsley sprigs, if desired, and serve hot. Makes 4 servings.

— VEGETARIAN LENTIL MEDLEY —

2/3 cup whole green lentils
2/3 cup split peas
2-1/2 cups cold water
2 leeks, cut in 1/4-inch slices
2 zucchini, cut in 1/4-inch slices
2 carrots, thinly sliced
2 stalks celery, thinly sliced
1 onion, coarsely chopped
1 clove garlic, crushed
2 tablespoons ghee
1/2 teaspoon turmeric
1 teaspoon mustard seeds
2 teaspoons Garam Masala, page 12
Salt to taste
Fresh celery leaves
Lemon slices

Soak lentils and peas overnight. Drain lentils and peas and put into a saucepan. Add cold water, bring to a boil and boil 10 minutes. Add vegetables and garlic, cover and cook gently 10 minutes.

Meanwhile, melt ghee in a saucepan. Add turmeric, mustard seeds and Garam Masala and cook gently 2 minutes or until seeds begin to pop. Stir into lentil mixture and cook 15 minutes or until vegetables and lentils are tender and liquid has been absorbed. Season with salt. Garnish with celery leaves and lemon slices and serve hot. Makes 4 servings.

CHICKEN TANDOORI

1 teaspoon mustard powder
1 (2-inch) piece ginger root, peeled,
  chopped
1/2 teaspoon cumin seeds
1/2 teaspoon ground coriander
1/2 teaspoon turmeric
1 teaspoon lemon juice
1/4 teaspoon hot chili powder
2 teaspoons tomato paste
1/3 cup corn oil
2/3 cup plain yogurt
8 chicken drumsticks, skinned
Lemon and lime twists, if desired
Fresh parsley sprig, if desired

In a bowl, mix mustard, ginger, cumin, coriander, turmeric, lemon juice and chili powder.

Add tomato paste and oil, a little at a time, mixing well to form a smooth sauce. Add remaining oil and stir in yogurt. Prick drumsticks several times with a wooden pick and place in a shallow glass dish. Pour marinade over drumsticks and turn drumsticks in mixture. Cover and marinate in refrigerator.

Preheat broiler. Arrange drumsticks in a broiler pan and cook 30 to 35 minutes or until cooked through, turning and basting frequently to ensure even browning and cooking. Garnish with lemon and lime twists and parsley sprig, if desired, and serve hot. Makes 4 servings.

FALAFEL

1 (13-oz.) can garbanzo beans, drained
1 onion, cut in fourths
2 cloves garlic
4 slices fresh white bread, cubed
1/4 teaspoon cumin seeds
4 small dried red chilies, crushed
1 tablespoon chopped fresh parsley
Salt and freshly ground pepper to taste
1 egg, beaten
1/3 cup dry fine bread crumbs
Vegetable oil for deep frying
4 pieces pita bread, warmed
Shredded lettuce
Onion slices
Tomato slices

Process garbanzo beans, onion, garlic, bread, cumin and chilies in a blender or food processor until smooth, then spoon mixture into a bowl. Add parsley, salt, pepper and egg; mix well. Form in 8 balls and coat in bread crumbs. Flatten balls slightly to form oval shapes.

Half fill a deep fat fryer or saucepan with oil; heat to 375F (190C) or until a 1/2-inch cube of day-old bread browns in 40 seconds. Fry Falafel, a few at a time, 3 minutes or until golden brown. Drain on paper towels. Cut pita bread in half and open to form pockets. Put 1 Falafel into each pocket with lettuce, onion and tomato slices and serve hot. Makes 8 servings.

— CEYLONESE CHICKEN CURRY —

2 large onions
1 (2-inch) piece ginger root, peeled,
  chopped
2 cloves garlic, peeled
2 tablespoons water
5 tablespoons corn oil
2-1/2 to 3 tablespoons Curry Powder,
  page 12
1-1/2 pounds boneless chicken breasts,
  skinned
1-1/2 tablespoons all-purpose flour
1-1/2 cups chicken stock
2 stalks celery, sliced
1 red or green bell pepper, seeded,
  diced
1/2 teaspoon cumin seeds
3 ounces button mushrooms, if desired
3/4 ounce creamed coconut, chopped
2 tomatoes, peeled, seeded, sliced
Toasted shredded coconut
Fresh chervil sprigs, if desired

Cut 1 onion in fourths. In a blender or food
processor, process onion, ginger and garlic
until very finely chopped. Heat 3 tablespoons of oil in a saucepan. Add onion
mixture and Curry Powder and fry 2 minutes, stirring constantly. Cut chicken in
bite-size cubes and add to onion mixture.
Fry until chicken is seared. Stir in flour and
cook 1 minute. Stir in stock and bring to a
boil. Cover and simmer gently 15 minutes.

Meanwhile, peel remaining onion and separate in rings. Heat remaining oil in a skillet. Add celery, onion rings, bell pepper,
cumin seeds and mushrooms, if desired,
and fry gently 4 minutes. Add vegetable
mixture to chicken mixture and cook 15
minutes. Stir in creamed coconut. Add
tomatoes and heat through. Garnish with
shredded coconut and chervil sprigs, if desired, and serve hot. Makes 6 to 8 servings.

BARBECUE SAUCE

3 tablespoons corn oil
1 small onion, finely chopped
1 clove garlic, crushed
1/2 teaspoon dry mustard
2 tablespoons malt vinegar
1 tablespoon Worcestershire sauce
2 tablespoons light-brown sugar
3 tablespoons catsup
1/2 teaspoon chili seasoning
3/4 cup chicken stock
Fresh Italian parsley sprig, if desired

Heat oil in a small saucepan. Add onion and garlic and cook gently 2 minutes, stirring frequently.

Stir in mustard, vinegar, Worcestershire sauce, sugar, catsup, chili seasoning and stock. Bring to a boil.

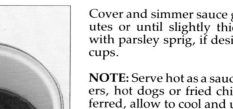

Cover and simmer sauce gently 7 to 8 minutes or until slightly thickened. Garnish with parsley sprig, if desired. Makes 1-1/4 cups.

NOTE: Serve hot as a sauce with hamburgers, hot dogs or fried chicken. Or, if preferred, allow to cool and use to brush over meats, poultry and fish while baking or grilling.

– WINE & PEPPER CREAM SAUCE –

2 tablespoons unsalted butter
2 shallots, finely chopped
1 tablespoon brandy
1/2 cup dry white wine
1/2 cup chicken stock
2 teaspoons green peppercorns,
   coarsely crushed
3 tablespoons whipping cream
1 tablespoon chopped fresh parsley
Fresh parsley sprig, if desired

Melt butter in a skillet. Add shallots and cook gently 3 minutes. Add brandy to pan and allow to heat through a few seconds, then flame. When flames subside, add wine to shallots.

Stir in stock and peppercorns and boil rapidly 2 to 3 minutes or until slightly reduced.

Remove from heat and stir in cream and chopped parsley. Return to medium heat and heat through 2 to 3 minutes, stirring constantly. Garnish with parsley sprig, if desired. Makes 3/4 cup.

NOTE: Serve hot with steaks, veal or fish dishes.

INDIAN MAYONNAISE DRESSING

1 tablespoon corn oil or ghee
1 small onion, finely chopped
2 teaspoons Curry Powder, page 12
1/4 teaspoon cayenne pepper
1 (1/2-inch) piece ginger root, peeled,
   chopped
2/3 cup mayonnaise
1 tablespoon tomato paste
1 tablespoon Mango Chutney, page 89
3 tablespoons half and half or plain
   yogurt
Cucumber slices, if desired, cut in half
Cucumber skin strips, if desired
Fresh parsley sprig, if desired

Heat oil or ghee in a saucepan. Add onion, Curry Powder, cayenne and ginger and cook gently 5 minutes, stirring frequently. Remove from heat and cool.

In a blender or food processor, process cooled onion mixture, mayonnaise, tomato paste, Mango Chutney and half and half or yogurt until smooth.

Turn mixture into a serving bowl. Chill at least 1 hour before serving. To serve, garnish with cucumber slices and skin strips and parsley sprig, if desired. Makes 1 cup.

NOTE: The consistency of this dressing may be thinned with the addition of a little more half and half or yogurt, if desired. Dressing will keep in a covered container in refrigerator for several days. Serve as an accompaniment to cold meats and salads.

—— SWEET SPICY CHILI SAUCE ——

1 clove garlic
1 Spanish onion, cut in fourths
2 fresh green chilies, seeded
2 tablespoons corn oil
1/2 teaspoon ground ginger
1 (8-oz.) can tomatoes in tomato juice
1/3 cup seedless raisins
1 tablespoon lemon juice
1 tablespoon dark soy sauce
2 tablespoons light-brown sugar
Salt and freshly ground pepper to taste
Fresh parsley sprig, if desired

In a blender or food processor, finely chop garlic, onion and chilies.

Heat oil in a saucepan. Add onion mixture and ginger and cook gently 3 minutes. Add tomatoes and break up with a spoon. Stir in raisins, lemon juice, soy sauce, brown sugar and water.

Bring to a boil, reduce heat and simmer 15 minutes, uncovered. Process in a blender or food processor to desired consistency. Reheat and season with salt and pepper. Garnish with parsley sprig, if desired. Makes 2-1/2 cups.

NOTE: Serve hot with grilled steak, fried chicken or grilled whitefish.

— TANGY MUSTARD SAUCE —

3 tablespoons butter
1 small onion, finely chopped
1/4 cup all-purpose flour
1 cup chicken stock
2/3 cup milk
1 bay leaf
1 teaspoon coarsely ground mustard
2 teaspoons dry mustard
1 tablespoon wine vinegar
1 teaspoon sugar
Salt and freshly ground pepper to taste
Additional fresh bay leaves, if desired

Melt butter in a saucepan. Add onion and cook gently 2 minutes. Stir in flour and cook 1 minute.

Stir in stock and bring to a boil, stirring constantly. Reduce heat and simmer 2 minutes, stirring constantly. Add milk and bay leaf, stir well and cook 2 minutes.

Blend mustards smoothly with vinegar and sugar. Add mustard mixture, salt and pepper to stock mixture and heat through 2 to 3 minutes. Remove bay leaf. Garnish with fresh bay leaves, if desired. Makes 1-3/4 cups.

NOTE: This recipe makes a thick sauce. If a thinner sauce is desired, add a little more stock or milk. Serve sauce hot with smoked sausage, rabbit and fish dishes.

- INDONESIAN COCONUT SAUCE -

1 cup shredded coconut
1-2/3 cups boiling water
3 tablespoons corn oil
1 onion, cut in fourths, then in thin
    slices
1 clove garlic, crushed
1 tablespoon Curry Powder, page 12
1/2 teaspoon turmeric
1/2 teaspoon ground coriander
1/2 teaspoon hot chili powder
1 tablespoon cornstarch
1 tablespoon lemon juice
1 large tomato, peeled, seeded
1/2 small green bell pepper, seeded
Salt to taste

In a blender or food processor, process coconut and boiling water 45 seconds. Strain mixture through a fine sieve, pressing coconut firmly to extract all liquid. Heat oil in a saucepan. Add onion, garlic, Curry Powder, turmeric, coriander and chili powder and fry gently 3 minutes, stirring.

Add coconut milk and bring to a boil. Cover and simmer gently 5 minutes. Blend cornstarch and lemon juice until smooth and add to coconut mixture. Bring to a boil and cook 2 minutes, stirring constantly. Cut tomato and bell pepper in thin slivers and add to sauce. Cook gently 5 minutes. Season with salt. Makes 2-1/4 cups.

NOTE: Serve hot with grilled steak and chicken or stir-fry dishes.

– LEMON BUTTER HOLLANDAISE –

1/4 cup lemon juice
1 teaspoon black peppercorns
3 blades mace
2 large egg yolks
1/2 cup butter, room temperature
3 good pinches cayenne pepper
Lemon slice, if desired
Paprika

Put lemon juice, peppercorns and mace into a small saucepan. Bring to a boil and boil until liquid is reduced by half. In a bowl, combine egg yolks with 1 tablespoon of butter and beat well.

Strain hot lemon liquid into butter mixture, beating constantly with a wooden spoon. Place pan over a very low heat and gradually add small pieces of remaining butter, whisking well until sauce is thickened and smooth. (If mixture gets too hot at this stage it will curdle and separate. To prevent this from happening, keep removing pan from heat while beating in butter to ensure gentle cooking.)

Add cayenne pepper to sauce and mix well. Turn mixture into a warm serving dish. Garnish with lemon slice, if desired, and sprinkle with paprika. Makes 2/3 cup.

NOTE: This rich egg and butter sauce requires great care during cooking to achieve delicious results. Serve warm or cold with poached salmon, asparagus or globe artichokes.

— PIQUANT ORIENTAL SAUCE —

2 tablespoon corn oil
1 onion, cut in fourths, then in thin
 slices
1 carrot, cut in julienne strips
1/2 green bell pepper, seeded, cut in
 thin strips
1 (1-1/2-inch) piece ginger root, peeled,
 chopped
3 good pinches Five Spice Powder,
 page 12
1 (8-oz.) can pineapple slices
1 tablespoon sugar
1 tablespoon dark soy sauce
1 tablespoon dry sherry
1 tablespoon malt vinegar
1-1/2 tablespoons catsup
1 tablespoon cornstarch
2/3 cup chicken stock
Fresh pineapple leaves, if desired

Heat oil in a saucepan. Add onion, carrot, bell pepper and ginger and stir-fry 3 minutes. Add Five Spice Powder and remove from heat. Drain pineapple slices, reserving juice. Add enough water to make 2/3 cup liquid. Cut 2 pineapple slices in thin pieces; reserve remaining pineapple slices for another use.

In a bowl, mix together sugar, soy sauce, sherry, vinegar, catsup and pineapple juice. Add pineapple juice mixture and pineapple pieces to vegetables. Blend cornstarch smoothly with a little stock, then add remaining stock. Add stock to vegetable mixture and bring to a boil, stirring constantly. Reduce heat and simmer 2 minutes, stirring constantly. Garnish with pineapple leaves, if desired. Makes 2-1/2 cups.

NOTE: Serve hot with fried chicken, pork steaks or shellfish.

ROAST PEPPER RELISH

1 yellow bell pepper, seeded, cut
  in half
1 red bell pepper, seeded, cut in half
1 green bell pepper, seeded, cut
  in half
1 onion, cut in fourths, then in
  thin slices
1/3 cup corn oil
2 tablespoons lemon juice
1 teaspoon coarsely ground mustard
1 clove garlic, crushed
1/2 teaspoon Garam Masala, page 12
1-1/2 teaspoons sugar
Salt and freshly ground pepper to taste

Preheat oven to 400F (205C). Place peppers, cut-sides down, in a roasting pan.

Bake in preheated oven 30 minutes or until skins begin to blister and blacken. Cool peppers, then peel. Cut peppers in fourths and slice in thin strips. Put peppers into a shallow dish. Sprinkle with onion.

Combine remaining ingredients in a screw-topped jar and shake vigorously until well blended. Pour mixture over peppers and marinate several hours, stirring occasionally. Makes 4 servings.

NOTE: Store in refrigerator up to 3 days. Garnish with a fresh cilantro sprig, if desired and serve chilled as an accompaniment to game pies, cold meats or crusty bread and cheese.

MANGO CHUTNEY

3 barely ripe mangos
2 tablespoons corn oil
1 (3/4-inch) piece ginger root, peeled,
  chopped
1 clove garlic, crushed
1 teaspoon salt
1/2 teaspoon hot chili powder
1/4 teaspoon cumin seeds
1/2 teaspoon fenugreek
1-1/4 cups malt vinegar
1/2 cup seedless raisins
1 tablespoon lemon juice
1-1/2 cups light-brown sugar

Slice mangos in half by cutting lengthwise close to seeds on either side.

Peel and cut flesh in 1/8-inch-thick slices. Also cut away as much mango flesh as possible from around pits, without including any fibrous parts of pits. Heat oil in a large saucepan. Add mangos, ginger, garlic, salt, chili powder, cumin and fenugreek. Cook gently 2 minutes, stirring.

Stir in vinegar, raisins, lemon juice and sugar. Heat slowly to dissolve sugar. Bring to a boil and simmer, uncovered, 35 to 40 minutes or until liquid thickens and becomes syrupy and mangos look translucent, stirring frequently. Meanwhile, wash and rinse pint jars in hot soapy water; rinse. Keep hot until needed. Prepare lids as manufacturer directs. Ladle hot chutney into 1 hot jar at a time, leaving 1/4 inch headspace. Release trapped air. Wipe rim of jar with a clean damp cloth. Attach lid and place in canner. Fill and close remaining jars. Process 10 minutes in a boiling-water bath. To serve, garnish with parsley sprig and lemon peel, if desired. Makes 2-1/2 pounds.

PICCALILLI

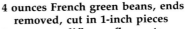

4 ounces French green beans, ends
    removed, cut in 1-inch pieces
8 ounces cauliflower flowerets
8 ounces small pickling onions, peeled
1 (8-oz.) piece cucumber, diced
1/2 cup pickling salt
1 teaspoon turmeric
1 tablespoon dry mustard
1/2 teaspoon ground ginger
1/3 cup sugar
1-3/4 cups distilled malt vinegar
4 teaspoons cornstarch

Layer all vegetables in a colander with salt.
Let stand overnight.

Wash 3 pint jars in hot soapy water; rinse.
Keep hot until needed. Prepare lids as
manufacturer directs. Rinse vegetables
well under cold running water and drain
thoroughly. Mix turmeric, mustard, ginger
and sugar with 1-1/2 cups vinegar and
blend well. Pour mixture into a saucepan
and add vegetables. Simmer gently 9 to 10
minutes or until vegetables are crisp-
tender.

Blend cornstarch to a smooth paste with
remaining vinegar. Add to vegetable mixture and mix well. Bring to a boil and cook 3
minutes, stirring carefully to prevent
damaging vegetables. Ladle hot relish into
1 hot jar at a time, leaving 1/4-inch headspace. Release trapped air. Wipe rim of jar
with a clean damp cloth. Attach lid and
place in canner. Fill and close remaining
jars. Process 10 minutes in a boiling-water
bath. Makes about 3 pints.

NOTE: Garnish with cucumber slices, if
desired, and serve with cold pies, salads
and sandwiches.

—— YOGURT TOMATO COOLER ——

1 tablespoon corn oil
2 cloves garlic, crushed
1/2 teaspoon cumin seeds
1 cup plain yogurt
1/2 teaspoon paprika
2 firm tomatoes, finely chopped
4 green onions, finely chopped
2 tablespoons chopped fresh mint
Salt and freshly ground pepper to taste
Fresh mint sprigs

Heat oil in a small saucepan. Add garlic and cumin seeds and cook very gently 2 minutes. Remove from heat and cool.

In a bowl, combine cooled garlic mixture, yogurt, paprika and stir well. Add tomatoes, green onions, chopped mint, salt and pepper.

Spoon mixture into a serving bowl and chill several hours. Garnish with mint sprigs. Makes 4 servings.

Variation: Omit tomatoes and onions and add 1 peeled seeded finely chopped or grated cucumber.

NOTE: Serve as an accompaniment to curries or as a tasty sauce with hot buttered Nan or pita bread.

—— PICKLED RED CABBAGE ——

1 (2-lb.) red cabbage
3 tablespoon pickling salt
2 tablespoons Pickling Spice, page 13
5 cups distilled malt vinegar
2 teaspoons caraway seeds

Cut cabbage in fourths and discard center stalk. Shred cabbage finely. Layer in a colander with salt and let stand overnight.

Put Pickling Spice and vinegar into a saucepan. Bring to a boil and boil 3 minutes. Remove from heat and cool. When cool, strain and reserve liquid. Meanwhile, wash 4 pint jars in hot soapy water; rinse. Keep hot until needed. Prepare lids as manufacturer directs.

Rinse cabbage well under cold running water. Drain thoroughly and mix with caraway seeds. Pack cabbage into hot jars. Pour cold spiced vinegar over cabbage to cover completely. Wipe rims of jars with a clean damp cloth. Attach lids and place in canner. Process 10 minutes in a boiling-water bath. Store in a cool dry dark place at least 5 days before serving. Makes about 4 pint jars.

NOTE: Use cabbage within 2 months; if left longer cabbage loses its crispness. Garnish with an Italian parsley sprig, if desired, and serve as an accompaniment to cold meats and poultry.

INDIAN APPLE CHUTNEY

1 pound cooking apples
1 pound onions, chopped
2 cloves garlic, crushed
3/4 cup golden raisins
2 teaspoons salt
1-1/2 cups sugar
2-1/2 cups malt vinegar
1/4 teaspoon cayenne pepper
1/4 teaspoon ground cumin
1/4 teaspoon ground ginger
1 teaspoon mustard seeds
1/4 teaspoon dry mustard
1 tablespoon tomato paste

Peel, core and coarsely chop apples.

Put apples, onions, garlic and raisins into a saucepan. Add salt, sugar, vinegar and spices and mix well. Heat gently, stirring to dissolve sugar.

Bring to a boil and simmer 30 minutes, stirring occasionally. Stir in tomato paste and continue cooking 7 to 8 minutes longer or until mixture is of a thick consistency with very little free liquid, stirring frequently. Meanwhile, wash 3 pint jars in hot soapy water; rinse. Keep hot until needed. Prepare lids as manufacturer directs. Ladle chutney into 1 hot jar at a time, leaving 1/4 inch headspace. Release trapped air. Wipe rim of jar with a clean damp cloth. Attach lid and place in canner. Fill and close remaining jars. Process 10 minutes in a boiling-water bath. Makes about 3 pint jars.

NOTE: This chutney improves if stored at least 3 weeks before serving. Garnish with an Italian parsley sprig, if desired, and serve as an accompaniment to curries or with crusty bread and cheese.

SPICY PICKLED PLUMS

2 pounds firm ripe plums
4 allspice berries
4 small dried red chilies
4 (1-inch) cinnamon sticks
6 whole cloves
4 blades of mace
3 cups distilled malt vinegar
3 cups sugar

Sterilize 2 quart jars. Keep hot until needed. Prepare lids as manufacturer directs. Prick plums several times with a cocktail stick. Half fill hot jars with plums.

Add 2 allspice berries, 2 chilies, 2 cinnamon sticks, 3 cloves and 2 blades of mace to each jar. Add remaining plums to fill jars. In a saucepan, combine vinegar and sugar and bring to a boil, stirring to dissolve sugar. Boil 5 minutes.

Pour hot vinegar into jars to cover plums completely. Wipe rims of jars with a clean damp cloth. Attach lids and place in canner. Process 20 minutes in a boiling-water bath. Store in a cool dry dark place at least 1 month before serving. Makes 2 quarts.

NOTE: Garnish with a fresh mint sprig, if desired, and serve with cold meats and salads.

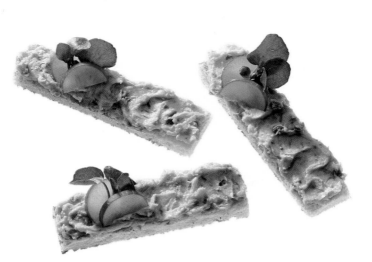

ANCHOVY SPREAD

1 (2-oz.) can anchovy fillets, drained
1 tablespoon milk
2 tablespoons butter, softened
1 ounce Bel Paese cheese
1 teaspoon lemon juice
3 pinches cayenne pepper
3 pinches ground nutmeg
1/4 teaspoon hot-pepper sauce
2 teaspoons capers, drained, finely
  chopped
Hot toast strips
Radish slices
Watercress sprigs

Put anchovies into a bowl with milk. Let soak 30 minutes. Drain well, then pat anchovies dry with paper towels.

Chop anchovies finely and put into a bowl with butter and cheese; mix well. Add lemon juice, cayenne, nutmeg and hot-pepper sauce.

In a blender or food processor, process to a smooth purée scraping mixture from sides of bowl occasionally. Add capers and mix well. Spread thinly on toast. Garnish with radish slices and watercress. Makes 4 to 6 servings.

NOTE: This mixture will keep in refrigerator up to 5 days.

—— WINE GLAZED ORANGES ——

1/2 cup sugar
3/4 cup water
3/4 cup red wine
4 whole cloves
2 teaspoons cassia bark, broken in
  small pieces
1 small piece dried ginger root
4 large oranges
Grated orange peel, if desired
Half and half

In a saucepan, combine sugar and water and heat slowly, stirring to dissolve sugar. Add wine, cloves, cassia bark and ginger. Bring to a boil and boil until slightly thickened and syrupy. Cool 5 minutes.

Meanwhile, using a sharp knife, peel oranges, removing all bitter white pith. Cut oranges in 1/4-inch-thick slices and place in a shallow dish. Strain wine syrup over oranges. Cover and chill several hours or overnight, turning slices occasionally in syrup.

Using wooden picks, secure orange slices together to form whole oranges and place in a serving dish. Pour wine syrup over oranges. Garnish with orange peel, if desired, and serve with half and half. Makes 4 servings.

NOTE: If desired, serve oranges in slices rather than as whole oranges.

— PEARS IN PINEAPPLE CREAM —

1 tablespoon lemon juice
4 large firm pears
4 pieces crystallized ginger, cut in
   halves
2 tablespoons butter
1 tablespoon light-brown sugar
2/3 cup pineapple juice
2/3 cup whipping cream
Fresh bay leaves
Toasted flaked almonds

Preheat oven to 375F (190C). Lightly grease a shallow baking dish. Fill a bowl with cold water and add lemon juice. Peel pears and cut in half. Cut away stems and remove cores with a teaspoon. Drop prepared pears in lemon water.

Pat pears dry on paper towels. Place a piece of crystallized ginger into "well" of each pear half. Arrange, pears, cut-sides down, in greased dish.

Put butter, brown sugar and pineapple juice into a saucepan and heat gently to dissolve sugar. Add whipping cream and boil 5 minutes. Pour sauce over pears. Cover and bake in preheated oven 1 hour or until pears are tender and sauce has thickened. Baste pears with sauce several times during baking. Place pears on a warm serving plate and spoon sauce over pears. Arrange bay leaves to resemble pear leaves and garnish with almonds. Serve hot. Makes 4 servings.

— MELON & GINGER BASKET —

1 large ripe honeydew melon
1/4 cup orange juice
1 to 2 pieces stem ginger, thinly sliced
2 tablespoons stem ginger syrup
Freshly grated nutmeg to taste
2 kiwifruit, peeled, cut in half, sliced
8 lychees, peeled, seeded
8 strawberries, cut in half
8 black grapes, cut in half, seeded
Fresh mint sprig, if desired
Ice cream

Cut a thin slice off one of rounded sides of melon (not pointed ends), so melon will sit level on a serving plate.

To form a handle, make 2 cuts about 3/4-inch wide on either side of a central strip. Continue cutting halfway down melon, then cut from bottom of handle around either side of fruit so these two wedges can be lifted away to form a basket shape. Cut away flesh from inside handle. Remove seeds from melon. Scoop out balls with a small melon scoop or cut flesh in pieces and place in a bowl. Smooth edge of melon basket.

Add orange juice, stem ginger and syrup and nutmeg to melon balls and stir lightly. Add kiwifruit, lychees, strawberries and grapes and mix lightly. Spoon mixture into melon and arrange fruits attractively. Cover and chill. Garnish with mint sprig, if desired, and serve with ice cream. Makes 4 to 6 servings.

Variation: Use fresh fruits such as cherries, pineapple, peaches, figs and nectarines. Substitute freshly squeezed lime juice for orange juice.

— LEMON GINGER SYLLABUBS —

1-1/4 cups whipping cream
1/3 cup sugar
Finely grated peel 1 lemon
2 tablespoons lemon juice
2 pieces stem ginger, chopped
1 egg white
2 kiwifruit, peeled, cut in fourths,
**   then sliced**
4 teaspoons stem ginger syrup
Lemon twists
Stem ginger slices
Cookies

Whip cream and sugar until cream begins
to thicken. Add lemon peel and juice and
whisk until thick and velvety.

Fold in stem ginger. Whisk egg white stiffly and fold into cream mixture. Place kiwifruit in bottom of 4 glasses. Sprinkle with
stem ginger syrup. Top with cream mixture and chill 2 hours.

Garnish with lemon and stem ginger.
Serve with cookies. Makes 4 servings.

Variation: Substitute pitted cherries, sliced
peaches or nectarines for kiwifruit.

— BERRIES WITH PEPPER SAUCE —

1 lemon
1 cup sugar
2/3 cup water
1-1/4 cups orange juice
1 tablespoon green peppercorns,
   coarsely crushed
1 pound strawberries
Fresh mint leaves, if desired
Half and half, if desired

Finely grate peel from lemon and put into a saucepan. Squeeze juice from lemon and reserve. Add sugar and water to lemon peel and heat gently, stirring until sugar dissolves.

Bring to a boil and boil until syrup turns a light caramel color. Remove from heat and hold pan handle with a cloth as mixture will splatter. Stir in lemon and orange juices. Heat gently, stirring to dissolve caramel.

Stir in peppercorns and boil 3 to 4 minutes or until slightly thickened and syrupy. Allow to cool 2 minutes, then spoon hot syrup over strawberries. Garnish with mint, if desired, and serve at once with half and half, if desired. Makes 4 servings.

GLAZED APPLE TART

1-1/2 cups all-purpose flour
Pinch salt
1/2 cup butter
3 tablespoons sugar
1 egg yolk
2 teaspoons cold water
4 Granny Smith apples
Finely grated peel 1/2 lemon
1/2 teaspoon cornstarch
1/2 teaspoon ground cinnamon
2 pinches ground nutmeg
5 tablespoons apricot jam
2 tablespoons lemon juice
Whipped cream
Fresh mint sprigs, if desired

Preheat oven to 375F (190C). Butter an 8-inch-round baking pan. To make pastry, sift flour and salt into a bowl. Add butter and cut in finely until mixture resembles bread crumbs. Stir in 1 tablespoon of sugar, egg yolk and cold water.

Knead gently until smooth and chill 15 minutes. Sprinkle with remaining sugar. Peel, core and cut apples in fairly thin slices. Arrange a layer of apple slices in overlapping circles in bottom of pan.

Mix remaining apple slices with lemon peel, cornstarch and spices. Spoon on top of arranged apple slices. Roll out pastry to a 8-inch circle. Place on top of apples and press gently. Prick several times with a fork. Bake in preheated oven 40 minutes or until pastry is golden brown. Carefully turn out tart onto a warm serving plate. Combine jam and lemon juice in a sauce-pan and heat gently until melted, stirring until smooth. Spoon hot jam mixture over tart. Serve hot or cold with whipped cream. Garnish with mint sprig, if desired. Makes 6 to 8 servings.

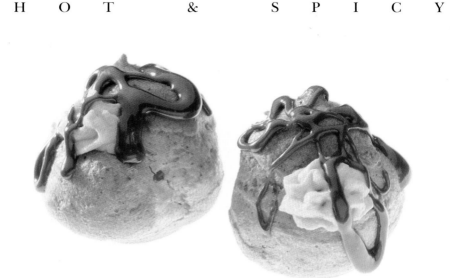

− CHOC 'N' SPICE PROFITEROLES −

1/2 cup plus 2 tablespoons all-purpose
 flour
1 teaspoon ground cinnamon
2/3 cup water
1/4 cup plus 1-1/2 teaspoons butter,
 diced
2 eggs, beaten
1-1/4 cups whipping cream
1 tablespoon powdered sugar
2 teaspoons coffee flavoring
4 ounces semisweet chocolate, broken
 in pieces
2 tablespoons Tia Maria
2 tablespoons light corn syrup
2 teaspoons superfine sugar

Preheat oven to 400F (205C). Lightly grease
several baking sheets.

Sift flour and 1/2 teaspoon of cinnamon
onto waxed paper. Pour water into a saucepan. Add 3-1/2 tablespoons butter and heat
gently until butter melts. Do not allow
water to boil before butter melts. Rapidly
bring to boil, remove from heat and add
flour all at once. Using a wooden spoon,
stir quickly to form a smooth mixture. Return pan to medium heat a few seconds
and beat well until dough forms a smooth
ball and leaves sides of pan clean.

Remove from heat and cool slightly. Gradually add eggs, a little at a time, beating
well after each addition to form a smooth
shiny dough. Transfer dough to a pastry
bag fitted with a 3/4-inch plain tube. Pipe
24 small balls onto greased baking sheets.

Bake in preheated oven 20 minutes, then reduce oven temperature to 350F (175C) and continue cooking 15 to 20 minutes longer or until well risen, crisp and sound hollow when tapped on bottoms. Make a slit in side of each pastry to allow steam to escape. Cool on a wire rack.

Whip cream, powdered sugar and coffee flavoring until thick. Spoon into a pastry bag fitted with a small star tube. Pipe cream into pastry or use a teaspoon to fill pastry with cream. Arrange profiteroles in a pyramid-shape on a serving dish.

Melt chocolate and remaining butter in a heatproof bowl set over a pan of gently simmering water. Stir in Tia Maria and corn syrup and continue stirring until sauce is smooth and coats back of a spoon. Spoon chocolate sauce over profiteroles and let stand a few minutes. Mix remaining 1/2 teaspoon of cinnamon with super-fine sugar and sprinkle over profiteroles. Makes 6 servings.

NOTE: Porfiteroles are at their best served 2 hours after assembling when they have softened slightly.

BAKLAVA

1/4 cup sugar
1-1/3 cups blanched chopped almonds
3/4 cup chopped walnuts
1-1/2 teaspoons ground cinnamon
1/2 teaspoon Mixed Spice, page 13
1 pound filo pastry
1 cup unsalted butter, melted
1-1/2 cups sugar
1-1/3 cups water
4 large pieces cassia bark
6 whole cloves
Lemon peel strip
2 tablespoons honey

In a bowl, combine 1/4 cup sugar, almonds, walnuts, cinnamon and Mixed Spice.

Preheat oven to 325F (165C). Grease a 13" x 9" baking pan. Line bottom of pan with a sheet of filo pastry, trimming it to fit. Brush with melted butter and add another 7 sheets of filo, trimming and brushing each one with butter before adding next sheet. Sprinkle half of nut mixture over filo, then cover with 4 sheets of filo, trimming and brushing each one with melted butter. Sprinkle remaining nut mixture on top and cover with 5 more sheets of filo, trimming and brushing each one with melted butter. Spread any remaining butter on top.

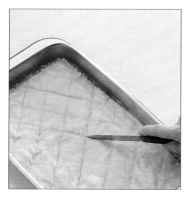

Using a sharp knife, cut through top layers of pastry, first one way, then the other, to make 25 diamond-shaped pieces. Bake in preheated oven 1 hour or until golden brown. If necessary, cover with foil during cooking to prevent overbrowning. Cool in pan. Combine 1-1/2 cups sugar and water in a large saucepan. Add cassia bark, cloves, lemon peel and honey and heat gently, stirring to dissolve sugar. Boil 5 minutes, then strain warm syrup over filo and let stand overnight. Makes 25 pieces.

—— CORNISH SAFFRON CAKE ——

3 (0.05 gram) packets saffron strands
1 tablespoon boiling water
1/3 cup sugar
1 cup warm water (110F/44C)
1 (1/4-oz.) package active dried yeast
 (about 1 tablespoon)
5 cups bread flour
1/4 teaspoon salt
3/4 cup lard
1/2 cup butter
1-2/3 cups currants or mixed fruit

Lightly grease 2 (9″ x 5″) loaf pans. Line a broiler pan with foil. Place saffron on foil and spread thinly. Place pan under a very low broiler and gently dry saffron (do not discolor) 3 to 4 minutes or until dry.

Place saffron in a small bowl and crush to a fine powder. Add boiling water and let stand 8 hours. Dissolve 1 teaspoon of sugar in 1/4 cup warm water. Add yeast, whisk and let stand 10 to 15 minutes or until frothy. Put flour, salt, lard and butter into a bowl and cut fats in finely. Mix in remaining sugar and currants. Stir saffron into remaining warm water and add to flour mixture. Stir in yeast and mix to form a dough. Knead lightly, cover and let rise in a warm place until double in bulk.

Knead dough and divide in half. Press each piece to a rectangle with width equal to length of loaf pan. Roll up dough, jelly-roll style, and place in greased loaf pans, seam side down. Press to fill corners. Cover and let stand at room temperature until dough has risen to top of pans. Preheat oven to 375F (190C). Bake in preheated oven 35 to 45 minutes or until golden. If necessary, cover with foil during baking to prevent overbrowning. Cool on a wire rack. Let stand 1 day before serving. Makes 2 cakes.

FROSTED GINGERBREAD

2 cups all-purpose flour
1/4 teaspoon salt
1/2 teaspoon Mixed Spice, page 13
1-1/2 teaspoons ground ginger
1 teaspoon baking soda
1/4 cup light corn syrup
1/4 cup molasses
1/3 cup hard margarine
1/2 cup dark-brown sugar
2 eggs, beaten
1 cup milk
1 (3-oz.) package cream cheese,
  softened
1 cup powdered sugar
Crystallized ginger slices

Preheat oven to 325F (165C). Grease an
11"x 7" baking pan. Line bottom and sides
with greased waxed paper, allowing paper
to stand 1-inch above sides of pan. Sift
flour, salt, Mixed Spice, ginger and baking
soda into a bowl. In a saucepan, combine
corn syrup, molasses, margarine and
brown sugar and heat gently until melted.
Stir into flour mixture and add eggs and
milk. Stir until evenly mixed.

Pour into prepared pan and bake in preheated oven 45 to 50 minutes or until well
risen and baked through. Cool in pan, turn
out and remove waxed paper. To make
icing, put cream cheese into a bowl and
soften well. Gradually sift powdered sugar
into cream cheese and mix well, using a
fork, to make a soft creamy mixture.
Spread icing over cold cake. Using blade of
a knife, form a rippled effect on icing.
Decorate with crystallized ginger. Cut into
12 pieces. Makes 12 servings.

— JAMAICAN CHOCOLATE CAKE —

1-1/2 cups self-rising flour
1-1/2 teaspoons baking powder
1 teaspoon Mixed Spice, page 13
3/4 cup margarine, softened
3/4 cup superfine sugar
3 eggs
2 tablespoons unsweetened cocoa
   powder
2 tablespoons hot water
1/2 cup granulated sugar
2/3 cup water
2 (2-inch) cinnamon sticks
1/4 cup dark rum
2 tablespoons slivered almonds
6 ounces semisweet chocolate, broken
   in pieces
Whipped cream

Preheat oven to 325F (165C). Generously grease a 5-cup fluted or plain tube pan and dust lightly with flour. Sift flour, baking powder and Mixed Spice into a bowl. Add margarine, superfine sugar and eggs. Blend cocoa powder with hot water and add to flour mixture. Beat well with a wooden spoon 2 minutes or 1 minute if using an electric mixer. Turn mixture into prepared pan. Bake in preheated oven 1-1/4 hours or until well risen and cake begins to shrink from edges of pan. Carefully turn out cake onto a wire rack and cool.

Combine granulated sugar and 2/3 cup water in a saucepan. Add cinnamon and heat gently, stirring to dissolve sugar. Boil 5 minutes. Remove from heat, add rum and discard cinnamon. Place cake on a plate. Spoon syrup over cake and let stand 2 hours. Stud top of cake with almonds. Melt chocolate; carefully spoon over cake, spreading to give a smooth even coating. Let stand several hours. Pipe (with a pastry bag) whipped cream around bottom of cake. Makes 10 to 12 servings.

BRANDY SNAPS

1/4 cup butter
1/4 cup light-brown sugar
2 tablespoons light corn syrup
1/2 cup all-purpose flour
Pinch salt
2 pinches Mixed Spice, page 13
1/2 teaspoon ground ginger
1/2 teaspoon lemon juice
2/3 cup whipping cream
1 teaspoon powdered sugar
Few drops vanilla extract
24 small strawberries

Preheat oven to 325F (165C). Generously grease 3 baking sheets.

Put butter, brown sugar and syrup in a saucepan and heat gently, stirring until butter has melted and sugar is dissolved. Cool slightly. Sift flour, salt, Mixed Spice and ginger into mixture. Add lemon juice and stir well. Drop teaspoonfuls of mixture onto greased baking sheets, spacing them well apart to allow for spreading. Bake 1 baking sheet at a time in preheated oven 6 to 8 minutes or until golden. Let cool on baking sheet 2 minutes.

Using a palette knife, remove brandy snaps from baking sheet, 1 at a time, and roll around handle of a wooden spoon. Let set and remove from handle. Just before serving, whip cream, powdered sugar and vanilla until thick. Spoon whipped cream into a pastry bag fitted with a small star tube. Pipe whipped cream into ends of each brandy snap. Garnish with strawberries and serve at once. Unfilled Brandy Snaps can be stored in an airtight container up to 2 weeks. Makes 12 brandy snaps.

— GERMAN PEPPER COOKIES —

1 egg
1/2 cup granulated sugar
1 cup all-purpose flour
Pinch salt
1/2 teaspoon ground cinnamon
1/4 teaspoon ground white pepper
1/4 teaspoon Mixed Spice, page 13
1 tablespoon cornstarch
1/2 teaspoon baking powder
Finely grated peel 1 lemon
2 tablespoons chopped mixed
    candied peel
Powdered sugar, if desired

Whisk egg and granulated sugar until light and fluffy.

Sift flour, salt, cinnamon, white pepper, Mixed Spice, cornstarch and baking powder into egg mixture. Add lemon peel and candied peel and stir well. Chill 1 hour.

Preheat oven to 350F (175C). Lightly grease several baking sheets. Form mixture into 16 small balls and place well apart on baking sheets. Bake in preheated oven 20 minutes or until well risen and lightly golden. Cool on a wire rack. Sprinkle with powdered sugar, if desired. Store several days before serving to allow time for flavors to mellow. Makes 16 cookies.

—— PEANUT BUTTER COOKIES ——

1/2 cup margarine, softened
1/2 cup crunchy peanut butter
1/2 cup granulated sugar
3/4 cup light-brown sugar
1 egg, beaten
1-1/2 cups all-purpose flour
1/2 teaspoon baking powder
3/4 teaspoon baking soda
Good pinch salt
1/2 teaspoon Mixed Spice, page 13
1/4 teaspoon ground cinnamon
2 good pinches freshly grated nutmeg
Glacé cherry halves
Blanched almonds

Preheat oven to 375F (190C). Lightly grease 2 baking sheets. In a bowl, beat margarine, peanut butter, sugars and egg until well combined. Sift flour with baking powder, baking soda, salt and spices. Add to peanut butter mixture and mix well. Divide in 25 equal pieces and shape in balls. Place, spaced well apart, on greased baking sheets. Flatten to 2-inch circles by pressing several times with a fork, first one way, then the other. Place a glacé cherry half in center of 13 cookies and almonds on remaining 12 cookies. Chill 30 minutes.

Bake cookies in preheated oven 10 to 12 minutes or until cooked through, but not hard. Cool on baking sheets 5 minutes, then remove to a wire rack to cool completely. Store in an airtight container up to 2 weeks. Makes 25 cookies.

NOTE: These cookies should be slightly chewy in center. However, if you prefer them crisp, do not chill mixture.

ICED COFFEE CREAM

2 tablespoons instant coffee
4 teaspoons light-brown sugar
1/3 cup boiling water
1/4 teaspoon ground cinnamon
Few pinches Mixed Spice, page 13
2/3 cup cold water
1-1/2 cups chilled milk
1 teaspoon vanilla extract
5 tablespoons whipping cream
8 ice cubes
4 small scoops vanilla ice cream
1/2 teaspoon sweetened cocoa powder
4 (3-inch) cinnamon sticks
Lime slices, if desired
Grated chocolate, if desired

Dissolve coffee and brown sugar in boiling water. Add cinnamon and Mixed Spice.

Add cold water and stir well. Add milk, vanilla and whipping cream. Whisk lightly until evenly combined.

Put 2 ice cubes into each glass. Half fill with coffee mixture. Add a scoop of ice cream to each glass and top up with remaining coffee. Sprinkle with unsweetened cocoa powder. Garnish with cinnamon sticks, lime slices and grated chocolate, if desired. Serve at once with long-handled spoons. Makes 4 servings.

Variation: For a sweeter version, increase brown sugar to taste. If desired, top each with a little whipped cream.

GLÛHWEIN

1 orange
8 whole cloves
1-1/4 cups cold water
1/4 cup sugar
3 (3-inch) cinnamon sticks
Freshly grated nutmeg to taste
3 blades mace
4 cups red wine
8 to 10 orange slices
8 to 10 (3-inch) cinnamon sticks

Stud orange with cloves and put into a saucepan. Add water, sugar, cinnamon, nutmeg and mace.

Heat gently, stirring to dissolve sugar. Bring to a boil, then reduce heat and simmer 5 minutes.

Add red wine and heat through gently. Strain and serve hot in heatproof glasses. Garnish with orange slices and cinnamon sticks. Makes 8 to 10 servings.

—— PINA COLADA PUNCH ——

1 piece dried ginger root, bruised with
   spoon
1 tablespoon light-brown sugar
1 tablespoon cassia bark, broken in
   small pieces
2/3 cup water
2 China teabags
2/3 shredded coconut
1-1/4 cups boiling water
1-3/4 cups pineapple juice
2/3 cup light rum or gin
Crushed ice
Maraschino cherries
Fresh pineapple chunks
Fresh pineapple leaves, if desired

Put ginger, sugar and cassia bark in a saucepan. Add 2/3 cup water and bring to a boil. Cover and simmer 5 minutes.

Remove from heat and add teabags. Let stand 5 minutes, then strain into a bowl. In a blender or food processor, blend coconut and boiling water 1 minute. Let stand 5 minutes, then strain into tea mixture, pressing coconut to extract all moisture.

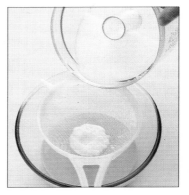

Add pineapple juice and chill 1 hour. Add rum or gin and stir well. Serve over crushed ice in tall glasses. Thread cocktail sticks with cherries and pineapple. Add a cocktail stick and swizzle stick to each glass. Garnish with pineapple leaves, if desired. Makes 4 to 6 servings.

Variation: Add more rum or gin for a stronger flavored drink.

NEGUS

1 bottle ruby port
1 tablespoon light-brown sugar
Finely grated peel 1 lemon
1/4 cup lemon juice
1/4 teaspoon freshly grated nutmeg
1/4 teaspoon ground cinnamon
4 whole cloves
2-1/2 cups boiling water
Thin strips lemon peel

Pour port into a saucepan and heat gently (do not allow to boil).

Add sugar, lemon peel and juice and spices. Stir well and simmer over a very low heat 10 minutes. Remove cloves.

Add boiling water and serve hot in heat-proof glasses. Decorate with lemon peel. Makes 10 to 12 servings.

——— HOT MULLED CIDER ———

1 large cooking apple
14 whole cloves
2/3 cup water
3 (3-inch) cinnamon sticks
6 allspice berries
1/4 teaspoon freshly grated nutmeg
2 tablespoons light-brown sugar
4 cups medium dry cider
2 tablespoons butter
Red apple slices
Fresh mint sprigs, if desired

Stud cooking apple with cloves. Cut apple in half and place, cut-sides down, in a saucepan. Add water, cinnamon, allspice, nutmeg and brown sugar.

Cover and simmer gently 20 minutes. Strain into a pan. Remove spices and press cooked apple through a sieve into pan.

Add cider and butter and heat through gently. Serve hot in heatproof glasses. Garnish with red apple slices and mint sprigs, if desired. Makes 8 to 10 servings.

GINGER BEER

**Finely grated peel and juice 1 large
    lemon
5 teaspoons cream of tartar
2 cups sugar
1 (1-inch) piece fresh ginger root
    (1 oz.), peeled
3 to 4 tablespoons dried ginger root
    (1 oz.)
8 cups boiling water
8 cups cold water
1 tablespoon cake compressed yeast
1 slice toast**

Place lemon peel, cream of tartar and sugar
in a large bowl or clean plastic bucket.
Crush fresh and dried ginger root with a
rolling pin and add to bowl.

Cover with boiling water and stir well until
sugar dissolves. Add cold water and lemon
juice and stir well. Spread yeast on toast
and float (yeast-side down) on mixture.
Cover with a clean cloth and let stand in a
warm place 24 hours.

Strain ginger beer through muslin. Pour
into clean plastic bottles, filling each half-
full (this allows room for mixture to effer-
vesce upon opening). Screw lids on tightly
and let stand in a cool place 2 to 3 days.
Open each bottle to allow excess air to escape and replace lids. Drink Ginger Beer
within 2 weeks. Makes 15 to 20 servings.

NOTE: To crush dried ginger root, place in
a plastic bag and crush with a rolling pin on
a flat surface. To serve, garnish with fresh
mint sprigs, lemon pieces and lemon peel
strips, if desired.

SHERBET

1-3/4 cups water
1 cup sugar
2 (3-inch) cinnamon sticks
1/2 teaspoon whole cloves
8 green cardamoms, lightly crushed
3 lemon peel strips
1/2 teaspoon rose water
1 to 2 drops red food coloring, if
  desired
Ice cold water
Lemon peel curls
Rose petals

Pour water into a saucepan. Add sugar, cinnamon, cloves, cardamoms and lemon peel. Heat gently, stirring to dissolve sugar.

Bring to a boil, then reduce heat and simmer gently 20 to 30 minutes or until mixture is thickened and syrupy. Remove from heat.

Stir in rose water and food coloring, if desired. Strain and cool, then dilute with ice-cold water. Serve in glasses, garnished with lemon peel and rose petals. Makes 6 to 8 servings.

SWEET LASSI

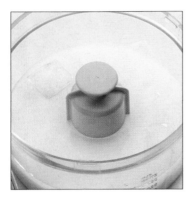

1-3/4 cups plain yogurt
4 ice cubes
1-1/4 cups ice cold water
2 teaspoons lemon juice
2 tablespoons sugar
Ice cubes
1/2 teaspoon cumin seeds, crushed
Lemon slices
Fresh mint sprig, if desired

In a blender or food processor, blend yogurt, 4 ice cubes and ice cold water 30 seconds.

Add lemon juice and sugar and blend mixture again until thoroughly combined.

Pour mixture over ice cubes in glasses and sprinkle with crushed cumin seeds. Garnish with lemon slices and mint sprig, if desired. Makes 6 servings.

— AUSTRIAN CHOCOLATE CUP —

**3 ounces semisweet chocolate, broken
   in pieces
Finely grated peel 1 small orange
1/4 teaspoon ground cinnamon
1-1/2 cups milk
1/4 cup whipping cream
Grated chocolate
2 to 3 (3-inch) cinnamon sticks**

Combine chocolate, orange peel, cinnamon and 3 tablespoons of milk in a saucepan and heat very gently until chocolate
melts, stirring frequently.

Add remaining milk and heat through
gently until piping hot, stirring frequently.
Whisk whipping cream until soft peaks
form.

Pour hot chocolate into mugs or heatproof
glasses. Top with whipped cream. Sprinkle with grated chocolate and add a cinnamon stick to each one for stirring. Makes 2
to 3 servings.

NOTE: Wind a curly strip of orange peel
around cinnamon sticks for a pretty effect,
if desired.

INDEX